THE COLONIAL CONSTITUTION

THE COLONIAL CONSTITUTION

ARGHYA SENGUPTA

juggernaut

JUGGERNAUT BOOKS
C-I-128, First Floor, Sangam Vihar, Near Holi Chowk,
New Delhi 110080, India

First published by Juggernaut Books 2023

10 9 8 7 6 5 4 3 2 1

P-ISBN: 9789353451929
E-ISBN: 9789353451790

Typeset in Baskerville Display PT by R. Ajith Kumar, Noida

Printed at Thomson Press India Ltd

Dedicated to my mother,

who loves India and strives to make it better every day

Contents

PROLOGUE

Vaishnava Jana To

The Constitution of India is a colonial document.

Sakala log ma sahune vande, ninda na kare keni re
Vach, kach, mann, nishchal raakhe, dhan dhan janani teni re

The one who respects everyone in the world, and speaks ill of none,
Who is unwavering in speech, action, and thought, blessed, blessed is his mother![1]

As Shakuntala sits down with child widow Chuiya to listen to Mahatma Gandhi's sermon at Rawalpur Cantonment railway station, the noise of the station gives way to the words of the Mahatma's favourite bhajan. Be respectful, be truthful, be virtuous, the poet Narsi Mehta writes. Shakuntala, moved by his words, rushes to put Chuiya on the train. 'Please take her to Gandhiji,' she beseeches his companions while handing her over. As the train disappears into the distance, Shakuntala looks on wistfully. She isn't sure of its destination but is certain that it is headed away from the discrimination, prejudice, and captivity that widows face in orthodox Hindu society.

Chuiya deserves a better life, like any ordinary eight-year-old. It is in Gandhi's vision of a kind, compassionate, truth-loving, and free India that Shakuntala hopes Chuiya will find her freedom.

This is the last scene of Deepa Mehta's *Water*, chronicling the lives of widows in Benares (Varanasi). It released in India in 2007, sixty years after Independence. It was in the making for over eight years, an unusually long time. In early 2000, when Mehta and her crew began shooting for the film in Benares, they were forcibly prevented from doing so. The government refused permissions, local groups claimed the film offended Hindu tradition and sentiment, the crew faced threats to their physical safety. Left with no option, in Benares or elsewhere in India, Mehta and her crew shot the film a few years later in Sri Lanka. It appeared that the words of Gandhi's favourite bhajan had fallen on deaf ears.

Around the same time as Mehta was besieged in Benares, in nearby New Delhi, India was celebrating fifty years of its Constitution. In a series of functions in the solemn yet celebratory atmosphere of the Supreme Court, dignitaries paid homage to the greatness of the Constitution. Indians quoted their British counterparts and vice versa in a feeling of mutual bonhomie. President K.R. Narayanan recalled the words of British judge Lord Woolf: 'The depth of feeling in India for the traditions of the common law has been astonishing and the richness of its development year by year has been helped by the excellent judges of the Indian Supreme Court.'[2] Lord Bingham, senior law lord, quoted India's first attorney general, M.C. Setalvad, to emphasize how the two legal systems were joined at the hip: 'The builders of the Indian Constitution not only drew largely from the collection of British ideas and institutions which was India's heritage from British rule, but they also took care to maintain a continuity with the Governmental system which had grown up under the British.'[3] It was a mutual love fest.

The leaders of the Indian freedom struggle had made a conscious design choice. The drafting of the Constitution of India was left to experts well versed in the law and comparative constitutional practices of Western democracies. Though the drafting started during the final year of India's freedom struggle, it remained surprisingly insulated from it. The philosophical basis of the freedom struggle was non-violence, yet the word 'non-violence' did not find mention in the Constitution. The most commonly used method to articulate this philosophy of non-violence was satyagraha, yet neither satyagraha nor truth-seeking were made central to the constitutional scheme. The freedom to criticize governments was a cherished goal of the struggle for independence, yet once India was free, the Constituent Assembly refused to outlaw the crime of sedition explicitly. The colonial masters may have returned to England, but colonial rule had not gone with them.

The Constitution, for India's leaders, was a technical document that would set out the basic structure of democratic government in an independent Indian republic. That government would have to be empowered to secure justice, liberty, equality, and fraternity for all its citizens. This would happen not through moral platitudes to citizens to do good, but rather through institutional structures designed to secure good governance.

There is much to be applauded about this constitutional vision. The framers of the Constitution were erudite, open-minded individuals who did not let the heady atmosphere of nationalism interfere overly with the structures of government India needed as an independent republic. They looked to advanced democracies to assess what had worked, spent time in trying to adapt those practices to Indian conditions, and unhesitatingly continued those structures of the colonial state that could be repurposed in independent India. The Federal Court, the somewhat titular apex court in colonial India, became the powerful Supreme Court of India, the Indian Civil Service (ICS), a unified national bureaucracy, became the Indian Administrative Service, and the Government of India Act, 1935, enacted by the United Kingdom parliament, became the basis for the Constitution of India. Key demands of the freedom movement – political rights for Indian citizens, structures for economic democracy, universal adult suffrage, and guaranteed safeguards for Scheduled Castes and Tribes – were incorporated constitutionally. The framers were not content merely declaring their goal of 'Justice, Liberty, Equality, and Fraternity' but laid out, in painstaking detail, the institutions that would take India there.

Equally, there was much that was disappointing about the Constitution. It was an extraordinarily long document, written in large part in dense, legal jargon. An ordinary citizen could neither make sense of large parts of it nor was it likely to be of much interest to them. It may have captured some of the demands of the freedom movement in terms of rights but had chosen not to channel its spirit of questioning the fundamentals of colonial rule: a large, all-powerful state with an overriding Union government. Instead, its key animating spirit was that if colonial institutions were now run *by* Indians, they would be run *for* Indians. The rest, as the framers repeated time and again, would depend on how the men and women who were chosen to operate the Constitution conducted themselves. 'Indeed, if I may say so, if things go wrong under the new Constitution the reason will not be that we had a bad Constitution. What we will have to say is that

Man was vile . . .'[4] said B.R. Ambedkar while presenting the draft Constitution to the Constituent Assembly.

To believe that man would be anything but vile was an optimistic foundation on which to frame a constitution. The United States, from which Ambedkar derived much inspiration, built its entire constitutional framework based on the view that the vile ambition of men (only men figured in the imagination of the framers of the US Constitution) would have to be counteracted by the equally vile ambition of other men through a complex scheme of checks and balances. Men could not be trusted to do the right thing. Gandhi believed that the focus of the nation state ought to be the moral and spiritual uplift of individuals; only then could the nation achieve its goals. But the framers of the Constitution thought otherwise: if newly independent Indians were given charge of their own destinies, they would certainly do right by themselves, their fellow citizens, and the Constitution.

This was an offshoot of the heady mixture of patriotism and optimism that was all-pervasive in newly independent India. There was the obvious promise of what a new, independent government backed by a new, sovereign constitution could achieve. For them, it was the fact of a constitution, put together in a short span of time, that ought to make Indians proud and hopeful. India taking its rightful place amongst the constellation of great nations in the world was a stated aim in the Objectives Resolution, the precursor to the Preamble to the Constitution of India. With the Constitution, explicitly inspired by the Declaration of the Rights of Man and following the basic framework of the Westminster form of government, India had arrived, speaking the language of global constitutionalism.

Over time, this narrative of India as an old democracy with a new, state-of-the-art constitution has crystallized into dogma. Commentators have heaped praise on the Constituent Assembly for borrowing liberally from foreign constitutions to give India a constitution that is 'both a declaration of social intent' and an 'intricate administrative blueprint'.[5] The Supreme Court, time and again, has underlined the greatness of the Constitution and its drafters. In the landmark *Kesavananda Bharati* case, where the court held that certain basic foundations of the Constitution could not be amended by Parliament, it also remarked, 'Our Constitution is unique.'[6] At other times, it has described the Constitution as the 'codified representation of the great spirit of Justice itself'.[7]

This outlook has been buttressed by hagiographic accounts of the Constitution by scholars. While one describes the Constitution as the 'founding moment',[8] another emphasizes its 'transformative'[9] potential.

Neither is wrong in a factual sense: the Constitution as a matter of fact did lay some sort of foundation for India as a republic with the fond hope that it would transform the suffocating atmosphere of colonial rule by providing fertile ground for freethinking citizens. But if Deepa Mehta's travails in Benares are any indication, the Constitution has not fulfilled this purpose. When free-thinking filmmakers clashed with staunch defenders of tradition, the constitutional state stood silently by.

It might be tempting to dismiss this failing with the assertion that man is, after all, vile. But there is a less speculative explanation: the Constitution of India is a colonial document. It is colonial for the simple factual reason that it is heavily borrowed from the Government of India Act, 1935, a fact that has been widely glossed over. Nearly two-thirds of the first draft of the Constitution of India presented to the Constituent Assembly and one-third of the final draft finalized by the Assembly were directly borrowed, with minor modifications where necessary. The basic set-up of a Union government in New Delhi and state governments in state capitals continued, as did the three organs of government: an elected legislature, a government headed by a prime minister or chief minister, directly answerable to the legislature, and the judiciary to resolve disputes. While in each of these matters, the Constituent Assembly made some significant changes, it did not tinker with the founding ideals underlying these institutions.

But the Indian Constitution is colonial in a more conceptual sense: it sets up a government that towers over the citizen much like colonial governments tend to do. Amongst the various arms of the governmental machinery, it is the establishment in New Delhi that wields disproportionate power over the whole country, a phenomenon that has been politely referred to as the Constitution being 'quasi-federal'. States and local bodies, closer to the people, while invested with some powers, are relegated to playing second fiddle. The Constitution contains a natural conservatism around questions of law and order, investing police with wide powers to search, seize, and arrest, despite lofty proclamations of fundamental rights. It is no surprise that the state of Uttar Pradesh did little to come to Deepa Mehta's rescue. It simply wasn't expected, except in theory, to empower and protect citizens. The Gandhian dictum of respecting everyone has been long forgotten.

Where the framers strike out on their own is in their insistence that the Constitution needs to provide as much for the economic well-being of citizens as for their political empowerment. This is a bold constitutional vision: freedom of religion, speech, and protest are meaningless if the stomachs of citizens are empty, their throats parched. But even here, for all the rhetoric of a socialist state declaimed across the spectrum in the Constituent Assembly, lawyerly conservatism prevailed. Since provision of socio-economic rights such as work, education, and legal aid involved significant budgetary allocations, the framers of the Constitution, deferring to established wisdom, retreated from a position of high principle. Though these principles were declared to be 'fundamental to the governance of the country', they were considered 'directive principles', not enforceable in any meaningful way. Here too, the originality of their thought succumbed to the conservatism of established modes of thinking.

These established modes of thinking were widely shared by members of the Constituent Assembly. Ambedkar, as the chairman of the Drafting Committee, adroitly shepherded such thinking into coherent legal form. This has given rise to the impression that Ambedkar was solely responsible for the draft of the Constitution of India. This is entirely untrue. Ambedkar, based on his deep study of comparative constitutional law combined with being at the receiving end – for decades – of orthodox Hindu society's concept of untouchability, had definite views on how the citizen–state relationship should be structured. This aligned with how the majority of the Constituent Assembly also saw it – though their reasons were distinct.

But they shared the collective wisdom of the time that independent India needed a powerful state that would be empowered to shape the lives of citizens. Alternatives to the draft Constitution by ideologically distinct parties, be it the one authored by M.N. Roy that set up a large welfare state[10] or the draft prepared by the Socialist Party of India,[11] had significant similarities.

Also aligned with the fundamentals of the document was the All India Hindu Mahasabha. The constitutional vision of the Mahasabha was altogether reasonable: it advocated a secular state with no state religion and freedom of religion for all. It also demanded a strong Union government to curb secessionist tendencies that any regional or religious groups might have. Though Savarkar's theory of Hindutva ran counter to their own constitutional vision, for the Mahasabha, this was not a contradiction. Hindutva was first and foremost a doctrine for Hindu revivalism in society, to restore Hindu self-worth. To achieve this required work outside the Constitution and the state, not inside it.

The growth of such work remained stunted because of the larger-than-life presence of Mahatma Gandhi. Here was an avowed secularist who came across as the epitome of holiness – dressed like a sadhu, professing his love for Meera bhajans, and declaring the establishment of Ram Rajya as his political objective. Like the adherents of Hindutva, Gandhi too was not focally interested in the Constitution at the time it was being drafted. His physical absence from the Constituent Assembly as well as his intellectual remoteness from questions of constitutional law meant that the draft Constitution did not have any ideological competition. This was one of the key reasons why the Constitution, according to noted Gandhian Kengal Hanumanthaiah, resembled the 'music of an English band'.[12]

The Colonial Constitution is the story of why a group of freedom-loving Indians who, having liberated themselves after two centuries of colonial rule, chose to compose this so-called music of an English band and call it the Constitution of India. It is a tale of texts that they looked up to as models and contexts of the fluid nature of Indian politics at the time of the country's independence and partition. It features the most outstanding political leaders of the generation displaying both exalted erudition and banal sentiment, dashes of originality interspersed with episodes of cautious copying. It is neither a celebration of the Constitution nor a critique. It is an origin story that begins on the morning of April Fools' Day, 1937.

PART I

DECISIONS

ONE

Mangu's Angst, Macaulay's Pride

The framers of the Constitution wanted consensus. They thought that an Indianized version of the Government of India Act, 1935, was the best way to achieve it.

For Ustad Mangu, the tongawalla, the Government of India Act, 1935, was the new constitution that would change everything. It would be the hot water in which rich moneylenders who sucked the blood of the poor would be boiled. The British 'white mice' would be swept away and forced to burrow into their holes underground. At last, Indians like himself and his fellow tongawallas would be free.

The Government of India Act came into existence on 1 April 1937. On the same day, Mangu beat up a British soldier who had earlier insulted him grievously. His punches were accompanied by cries of 'new constitution, new constitution', 'it is we who are the Raj now'. Mangu was confident that in the new India, the ignominy of servitude was over. No more would there be tolerance towards insults by the British, no more servility towards colonial masters. A new dawn of freedom had arrived.

Mangu's mythical constitutional bubble lasted only a few minutes. He was promptly locked up. 'It's the same old constitution, you fool,' the constables laughed and told him. So much had changed, yet nothing seemed to have changed at all. The Act appeared to be a cruel April Fools' joke played on Mangu.

His betrayal by the Government of India Act was satirized poignantly by Saadat Hasan Manto in his short story 'Naya Kanoon'.[1] Its contents presumably didn't reach the drafters of the eventual Constitution of India.

The Government of India Act Redux

The Constituent Assembly, the body tasked with drafting the Indian Constitution, was made up by allocating to each province of British India a fixed number of seats in proportion to its population. Across all provinces, the total number of seats stood at 292. In each province, seats were further divided between the main communities in that province in proportion to their population: general (which included caste Hindus as well as Depressed Classes, those classes considered untouchable by the caste system), Muslims, and Sikhs (only in Punjab). The representatives of these communities would be elected only by those members of the provincial legislative assembly who also belonged to that community. For example, in the election to fill the four seats allotted to the Sikhs in Punjab, only Sikh members of the Punjab legislative assembly could cast votes. A total of ninety-three seats were also reserved for representatives of the princely states – which were filled through a variety of methods such as indirect election by legislative assemblies or purpose-built electoral colleges, direct nomination by the ruler, etc.[2]

The elections to fill the seats allotted to the provinces were completed by July 1947. The results were predictable. Of the 210 seats reserved for the general category, the Congress won 199, and of the seventy-eight seats reserved for Muslims, the Muslim League won seventy-three. Including some of the Sikh representatives and the representatives of three of the Chief Commissioner's Provinces – Coorg, Delhi, and Ajmer-Merwara – who were also Congressmen, the Congress tally in the Constituent Assembly stood at 208 – a little more than half the total membership of the Assembly.[3] To ensure that the membership of the Assembly was truly representative of the nation at large, the Congress had nominated members from all communities. Ultimately, out of the 208 Congress candidates who won, 29 were from the Scheduled Castes, 6 were Indian Christians, 3 were Anglo-Indians, 3 were Parsis, and 4 belonged to tribal communities.[4]

To make the best available talent a part of the drafting process, the Congress made sure to look outside the party for nominations. Ultimately, as many as thirty members who were elected on the Congress vote were not members of the party.[5] These included members such as B.R. Ambedkar, N.G. Ayyangar, A.K. Ayyar, S. Radhakrishnan, and H.N. Kunzru – stalwarts who went on to play a critical role in the drafting of the Constitution.

The actual task of drafting the Constitution took place in three phases. In the first phase between the end of 1946 and the middle of 1947, the president of the Constituent Assembly had set up twelve committees to prepare reports on salient features of the Constitution. This included the Union Powers Committee that would determine the powers of the Union government, the Advisory Committee that would finalize fundamental rights, and the Ad-hoc Committee on the Supreme Court that would lay down the powers of the new Supreme Court. Concurrently, B.N. Rau, the constitutional adviser, was given the task of sending out questionnaires to all serving members of provincial legislatures and the central legislature, as well as the Assembly, synthesizing their views with those contained in the committee reports and putting together the first draft of the Constitution. In the second phase beginning October 1947, this draft was sent to the Drafting Committee appointed specifically for the purpose of scrutinizing and revising Rau's draft to ensure that the views of the various committees had been incorporated and harmonized. The Drafting Committee, led by Ambedkar, modified the first draft and presented its version to the entire Constituent Assembly for comments in February 1948. After the comments were duly considered, from November 1948, the Constituent Assembly began its third phase. This involved a clause-by-clause debate on its provisions for a year, till the draft Constitution was finalized in November 1949.

Called upon to draft a new constitution, the drafters naturally turned to the Government of India Act to adopt some of its provisions. Ambedkar was unapologetic:

> It is said that there is nothing new in the Draft Constitution, that about half of it has been copied from the Government of India Act . . . There is nothing to be ashamed of in borrowing. It involves no plagiarism. Nobody holds any patent rights in the fundamental ideas of a Constitution.[6]

From a draftsman's viewpoint, this was sensible. The Constituent Assembly was working under immense pressure of time to give India a constitution that would set the republic in motion. The more protracted the deliberations, the longer India would be governed by the British-enacted Government of India Act, 1935. If there were salutary provisions that had worked in the past, common sense demanded that such provisions be continued. But would it be a constitution that would work for Mangu and his fellow citizens of India? That would depend entirely on which provisions of the Government of India Act were being borrowed and how those would be adapted to independent India.

Enacted 'by the King's most Excellent Majesty' in 1935,[7] the Government of India Act had set up the basic structure of a federal government. Power would be divided between the Union government in New Delhi and provinces. In New Delhi, power would be shared between the governor-general who was the viceroy of India appointed by the British monarch and a legislature with two houses. The two houses, the Council of State and the Federal Assembly, would both have elected and nominated members. Nominations would be by the governor-general and elections would be held where all members of provincial legislatures could vote through communal electorates. This meant Hindus voted for Hindu candidates, Muslims for Muslim candidates, and so on. Princely states had separate representation. Despite this elaborate scheme to divide powers, the governor-general continued to remain all-powerful, with complete control over defence, foreign affairs, ecclesiastical matters, and tribal affairs. In all other matters too, he could issue ordinances, enact Governor-General's Acts which were similar to laws enacted by the legislature, and also take over the entire functioning of the government if he felt the government was not acting in accordance with law. Despite some self-government, there was no doubt that India was still ruled by a British governor-general.

Similarly, in the provinces, an unelected governor would notionally share power with a directly elected provincial legislature. Elections would be on the basis of a limited franchise consisting of only those who paid taxes, had passed their matriculation exam, or owned property. As a result, only 20–25 per cent of all Indian adults were eligible to vote.[8] Like the governor-general, the governors, also British appointees, had wide discretionary powers at the provincial level, including the authority to pass or veto bills at their discretion. A governor could also dismiss the elected government and take over all its functions when it was not functioning in accordance with law. This was consistent with the overarching design of the Act: it provided a whiff of self-government to colonized Indians that could quickly be retracted if the circumstances demanded.

The Government of India Act was certainly not what the freedom movement had aspired to. Its provisions ensured that India was neither a dominion nor did it have any meaningful attribute of national self-government. No provisions for citizenship were included and Indians remained subjects of the British empire. There were no fundamental rights and no obligations of the state worth the name.[9] The franchise in elections was restricted to the wealthy and educated; it was no more than a fig leaf. Communal electorates also meant that unity amongst Indian legislators was made difficult by design. If 'divide and rule' was the abiding philosophy of the British Raj, the Government of India Act was its legal avatar.

This is why Jawaharlal Nehru, in his presidential speech at the Lucknow session of the Congress in 1936, termed the Act a 'new charter of slavery' intended to 'strengthen the bonds of imperialist domination and to intensify the exploitation our masses'.[10] In the same session, Dr Rajendra Prasad introduced a resolution denouncing the Act as one that 'in no way represents the will of the nation, is designed to facilitate and perpetuate the domination and exploitation of the people of India'.[11] Madan Mohan Malaviya went further and declared that 'not only does [the Government of India Act] not give us freedom but it takes away what little freedom we have'.[12] Jinnah was dissatisfied with the vast majority of seats in legislatures having been given to Hindus and is said to have called it 'thoroughly rotten, fundamentally bad, and totally unacceptable.'[13]

Yet 150 out of 239 articles of the first draft Constitution of India written by Indians for independent India were based on, or copied from, the very same Government of India Act that had been so roundly denounced. This draft, put together by constitutional adviser Benegal Narsing Rau and the Constituent Assembly Secretariat, a temporary, specialized cadre of bureaucrats set up specifically to assist the Assembly in its functions, was presented to the Drafting Committee in October 1947. A significant portion of the Government of India Act made it, unchanged, to the final version of the Constitution adopted by the Assembly in November 1949. The cognitive dissonance was astounding.

A clause-by-clause comparison of the provisions of the Constitution of India and the Government of India Act brings out this remarkable similarity. Chapters on the Union and state executive, Parliament, State Legislatures, and the distribution of powers between them, key institutions and functionaries like the Supreme Court, high courts, the attorney general, the comptroller and auditor general and the processes relating to distribution of revenue, making of central grants, engaging in trade, commerce, and borrowing, and entering into government contracts are directly copied, with or without some modifications. Much of this can be attributed to the preference for familiarity in a fluid and fast-changing political atmosphere. But equally, the near-wholesale replication of the basic structure of colonial government meant that the framers had made a specific design choice. Independent India would inherit the institutions of a colonial state that were designed to rule from above. Power would be shared top-down between the Centre and the states. Checks and balances on them would be in the form of powerful constitutional courts and exalted constitutional authorities like the comptroller and auditor general. The president occupying the magnificent Rashtrapati Bhavan in New Delhi and governors in their majestic Raj Bhavans in state capitals would be the formal wielders of all sovereign power.

But why did India need a president in the first place? Could a poor country afford a governor in each state? Now that power had passed from colonial rulers to Indians themselves, why should the ICS, set up to create a class of professional administrators to perpetuate colonial interests, continue to manage matters of state instead of autonomous panchayats or local officers? Except in all-too-cursory allusions, none of these questions were meaningfully contemplated by the Constituent Assembly.

This was a missed opportunity. The chance to draft a new constitution is one that very few generations of political leadership get. Especially when accompanied by a momentous event like the emergence of an independent nation state, with the national mood rife with anticipation and hope for the future, writing a constitution is an opportunity to manifest that hope into a document to stand the test of time. It is a chance to ask fundamental questions about where the nation is headed and which political institutions would best take it there. Indian leaders had a clear sense of a nation that would be a sovereign, democratic republic. But first-order deliberations on the political institutions best suited to this objective were foreclosed by a ready draft law that was available. The tumult of the period immediately preceding Independence was such that the Constituent Assembly had more immediate priorities. Trying to keep the Muslim League mollified and ensuring the indivisibility of India were foremost amongst them.

Consensus and Continuity

In February 1946, Prime Minister Clement Attlee announced that a special mission of British cabinet ministers would be sent to India to help secure independence as soon as possible. The primary task of the Cabinet Mission as soon as it arrived in India was to bridge the differences between the Congress and the Muslim League and set up a Constituent Assembly to determine the future of India. For a few years, Jinnah and the Muslim League had demanded partition and the formation of two separate constituent assemblies – one for each independent dominion of India and Pakistan. But the Cabinet Mission Plan put paid to this demand.

The country would remain united with a limited central government. Provinces were to be grouped into three sections: those with a Hindu majority constituting most of the Indian land mass, those with a Muslim majority in the north-west of the country, and those with nearly equal representation in the east. An all-India Constituent Assembly consisting of provincial representatives would be convened to draft the Constitution of India as well as one for each group of provinces.

When the all-India Constituent Assembly convened in December 1946, the Muslim League was absent. Though it had been willing to go along with the Cabinet Mission proposals viewing 'the basis and foundation of Pakistan . . . inherent in the Mission's plan', difficulties arose in the establishment and operation of the coalition government of the Muslim League and the Congress to implement the plan. The Congress rejected the idea of the interim government since the viceroy had not included any Indian Muslim who did not belong to the Muslim League. This was unacceptable to the Congress's principled stand that the Muslim League alone did not speak on behalf of all Indian Muslims. Though the Muslim League had agreed to join the interim government, the viceroy postponed the plan. Jinnah protested and demanded that the establishment of the Constituent Assembly should also be delayed. But the viceroy refused. Elections were held to the Constituent

Assembly in July 1946. Furious efforts were still under way to convince the Muslim League to join the Assembly and the interim government. But though it joined the government, it never joined the Assembly.

This is why when the Assembly first met, with the seats of the Muslim League vacant, interspersed with the idealism of drafting a new constitution was the realization that it would have to be something akin to a common minimum programme that would be acceptable to the Muslim League. This is exactly how Gandhi had viewed the Constitution: not as a blueprint for the future but rather as a balm to heal differences and generate lasting consensus. In this context, making radical changes was anathema. Unsurprisingly, with the Government of India Act, 1935, available as an inherited text which all parties had worked with for the past decade, it was a natural choice as a base document. All parties were familiar with it, no party had a hand in making it directly: it was the least-worst option that had the best chance of being acceptable to all.

There was another reason why the Government of India Act formed the basis of Indian constitutional discussions. Benegal Narsing Rau had been appointed constitutional adviser to assist the Constituent Assembly in drafting the Constitution. Rau was uniquely suited to the task. A career bureaucrat who had later been appointed a judge of the Calcutta High Court, Rau was a model ICS officer. His erudition combined with considerable administrative nous meant that when the Government of India Act was enacted, Rau was appointed officer on special duty to the Reforms Office. In this role, he was expected to bring 1,500-odd laws in line with the Government of India Act, which, though technically just another law, was in some respects akin to a constitution according to which India was governed. It set up the legislature, the executive, and the judiciary at the Union and state levels, laid out their powers, obligations, and relationships. Rau certainly treated it as a constitutional document, much to the displeasure of his colleagues at the Reforms Office who saw it as just another law that was required to be harmonized with other laws.[14]

His considerable experience in dealing with the intricacies of the Government of India Act meant that when he was called upon to serve as the constitutional adviser, he knew where to look. Entrusted with circulating a questionnaire to all members of the central and provincial legislatures to elicit their views on various features of a proposed constitution, he presented a straightforward menu of choices.[15] Will the head of the Indian Union be a real head as in the United States of America or merely a nominal head as in Switzerland? Should the office rotate amongst different communities in turn like Switzerland, or should it happen organically like in Ireland? Should the Union executive be of the British type (parliamentary) or the American type (non-parliamentary) or the Swiss type (mixed) or any other type?

Each of these questions was derived from the Government of India Act. Rau sought to repurpose the arrangements under the Act in a manner that would promote Indian interests. This was technocratic constitution drafting at its best: adapting a familiar working framework rather than restarting from scratch, ensuring continuity rather than a decisive break from colonial institutions, deriving from best practices in other constitutions rather than creating new best practices that would work for India. This was the 'deep state' of India's constitutional drafting, making sure that the ultimate constitution never veered away too dramatically from tried-and-tested precedents.

Rau was helped by the fact that between 1935 and 1949, Indian politicians, civil servants, and judges had developed a working knowledge of the provisions of the Government of India Act. Following the coming into force of the Act, the Congress successfully contested the first provincial elections held in 1937 and went on to single-handedly form six provincial governments in Madras, Bihar, Orissa, Central Provinces, United Provinces, and Bombay. The Congress ministries exercised the powers available to them under the Government of India Act for a remarkably wide variety of purposes: from passing resolutions condemning the Act itself as an instrument designed to 'perpetuate the subjection of the people of India' because it failed to grant any semblance of self-government, to clamping down on popular agitations for the sake of 'defence of life and property', from passing social welfare legislation for the benefit of small landholders to prosecuting individuals for sedition. The experience of Congress men and women with self-government were based solely on the powers vested in them by the Government of India Act. The Muslim League too was fully familiar with its provisions, having administered Punjab, Bengal, and Sind by forming governments in those provinces after the mass resignation of Congress ministries in 1939 and after the League's own success in the 1946 provincial elections.[16]

Even during the process of drafting the Constitution, the Constituent Assembly, which functioned as the interim Parliament, operated the provisions of the Act side by side with its constitution-drafting responsibilities.[17] For members of the Assembly, continuing the provisions of the Government of India Act did not amount to copying from a colonial relic. It was rather a case of continuing business as usual.

A draft at least a third of which represented a business-as-usual structure of colonial government could hardly be said to be a decisive break from the past. But in one key respect, the game had changed. It was agreed early on in the Constituent Assembly that every adult Indian would now have the right to vote, irrespective of any property ownership or educational qualifications. This was a consistent demand of the Congress party and used to critique British constitutional reforms which made the right to vote conditional. Now that every single Indian, literate and illiterate, landed and landless, would have one vote each, the framers believed that the institutions that represented them would operate differently.

This was a fair assumption, given the heady political atmosphere of imminent freedom and the collective urge to build something new and beautiful. But when taken together with the fact that the institutions of government themselves were colonial conceptualizations designed to rule India from above, how would such a change ultimately work itself out when the atmosphere was less heady? This was an open question, one that the framers knew could not be taken for granted. To ensure that the promise of democracy lived on after the initial euphoria diminished, the structures of colonial government would now have to be Indianized.

Constitutional Hodgepodge

The moulding process of the Government of India Act to make it the Constitution of India was eclectic. Members drew on a range of experiences to shape a constitution that they believed would work best in India. Predominant amongst these experiences were examples of the actual working of constitutional provisions in other parts of the world. For the members of the Constituent Assembly, knowledge that a provision had worked elsewhere provided a useful basis to replicate such a provision in the Constitution of India. This was typical of a lawyer's reliance on strong precedents to build their argument. That this approach was adopted is hardly surprising, since every member who served on the Drafting Committee was a lawyer. Alladi Krishnaswamy Ayyar, N. Gopalaswami Ayyangar, Bhimrao Ambedkar, Kanhaiyalal Munshi, Syed Muhammad Saadulla, B.L. Mitter,[18] and Debi Prasad Khaitan[19] were all lawyers at least by training and most of them enjoyed thriving practices.

B.N. Rau's initial questionnaire to all members of the central and provincial legislatures set the tone. Each of the questions pertained to a central feature of the proposed constitution. For example, should the executive be directly elected? Should the legislature have one chamber or two? Should there be a separate chain of courts to administer Union laws?

These questions themselves were not freestanding. After each question, the comparative provisions in the constitutions of the United States, Switzerland, Ireland, Canada, Australia, and South Africa were provided. While this was ostensibly done to guide the members, it seemed like a menu of choices from which they could pick. Off-menu answers were unlikely, given the plethora of choices presented. Members were not asked for systems of government that might best solve specific problems in their constituency. Neither was their opinion sought on whether any model other than the one based on separation of powers between the legislature, executive, and the judiciary was appropriate for India. The parameters within which the Constitution of India would operate were set by operative constitutions in other parts of the world.

Within a week of Rau sending the questionnaire in March 1947, Ambedkar came up with his own set of draft articles on fundamental rights of citizens. His draft was closely and unapologetically modelled on the US Constitution. The numbering system of the US Constitution, with sections nested within articles was replicated; the objective of the Constitution was to 'form a more perfect union',[20] bodily taken from the first line of the Preamble of the US Constitution, and even the name of the country was written as the 'United States of India'.[21]

While Ambedkar's version had many similarities with

the US Constitution, he drafted two strikingly original provisions. One was a series of declarations on the economic character of the country – key industries would be owned and run by the state, agriculture and insurance would be state industries, and collective farms would be established by the state, underlining that India would be a socialist state. Curiously, this provision was styled 'Remedies against invasion of Fundamental Rights'.[22] In Ambedkar's view, a socialist state was best placed to ensure that fundamental rights of citizens were upheld. This was a deeply held understanding based on the belief that only if citizens were well fed and housed would rights such as free speech and expression, or freedom to trade, have any meaning. To the unemployed, the promise of a job, even if it prevented them from joining a union and exercising their fundamental right to associate with others, would be preferable to the theoretical freedom to speak. Without such economic cover, constitutional freedom would mean 'dictatorship of the private employer'.[23] For Ambedkar, only a socialist state could prevent this from happening and ensure liberty of the individual. Developments in Stalinist Russia and Maoist China a few years later may have tempered these views somewhat, but when this was written in 1947, his view captured the intellectual zeitgeist of the immediate post-war period.

Second was an elaborate set of safeguards for Scheduled

Castes. These took the form of a quota of seats in Parliament based on separate electorates, quotas in government and government services, and a settlement commission to hold uncultivated lands in trust for Scheduled Caste persons.[24] According to the terms of the Poona Pact that Ambedkar had concluded with Gandhi in 1932, separate electorates, by which Scheduled Caste persons voted exclusively for Scheduled Caste representatives, had been specifically rejected. But now they were making a comeback in Ambedkar's original formulation of an ideal constitutional framework. The drafting of the Constitution of India was a major constitutional moment, and Ambedkar intended to seize the day by providing Scheduled Castes a range of safeguards and protections that were earlier denied to them. No country in the world had such detailed provisions on minority protection as the draft Constitution of India envisaged by Ambedkar.

This dash of originality apart, Ambedkar's outlook on constitution formation, as noted above, was shaped significantly by what had worked in the United States of America. This was most starkly evident when on 4 November 1948 he addressed the Assembly while introducing the draft Constitution that he and his colleagues on the Drafting Committee had put together. The occasion was momentous: for the first time, the Assembly, and through it the nation, would be presented a draft that would form the base of a future constitution of an independent Indian republic. One may have expected rousing rhetoric, a clear-eyed espousal of what forms of government India needed, a vision for India's future. Instead, Ambedkar started defensively. He first attempted to distinguish the president of India from the president of the United States, lest the similarity in nomenclature led one to the erroneous conclusion that India had set up a presidential system of government where a president is elected directly by the people. Though the presidential system was stable because the executive was not answerable to the legislature on an everyday basis, Ambedkar also believed it to be less responsible, as presidents had a freer hand to do as they pleased. The Drafting Committee, he said, 'preferred more responsibility to more stability'.[25] This would only be possible in a parliamentary system of government, where people directly elected their own representatives to Parliament. In Ambedkar's mind, the parliamentary system was more responsible since individual parliamentarians were directly accountable to a small number of constituents. This was unlike the American presidential form, where despite having immense power, the president was accountable to the whole country, a fuzzy and ineffective way of ensuring responsible government in Ambedkar's view.

As if battling American phantoms in his own mind,

he then went on to distinguish India's federal structure from America's dual government structure. The Indian federation would have single citizenship, not dual citizenship of state and Centre. It would also be more tightly knit in contrast to the loose connections between states and the federal government in Washington, DC. Not content with this distinction, Ambedkar went on to explain the features of the Indian federation that differed from those of other federal constitutions, most notably the ones in Australia and Canada. The Indian Constitution, he argued, could become unitary when necessary, such as in times of war. This ensured flexibility, lacking in the Australian Constitution. At the same time, he pointed to a raft of provisions that allowed the Union parliament to legislate on state subjects. These, together with the Indian Administrative Service, the Supreme Court and high courts, and the uniform civil and criminal laws in the country, were unity-preserving devices, rare in other federations.

Ambedkar was candid about his approach of copying constitutional provisions from elsewhere and adapting them to an Indian context. 'The only new things, if there can be any, in a Constitution framed so late in the day are the variations made to remove the faults and to accommodate it to the needs of the country,' he stated matter-of-factly.[26] For Ambedkar, it had been two centuries since the American and French Constitutions had provided a template for future drafting of constitutional documents. 'One likes to ask whether there can be anything new in a Constitution framed at this hour in the history of the world,' he wondered.[27] It was no wonder then that, a few exceptions apart, the draft Constitution of India had little novelty or originality.

'A bit from here and a bit from there – it is a Pandora's box. This is what has been produced by our friend Dr Ambedkar!'[28] When presented in the house, Ambedkar's draft Constitution shocked a voluble cross-section of the membership of the Assembly. Two members, Hasrat Mohani who described the Constitution as 'a Pandora's box', and Damodar Seth, moved resolutions that a new Constituent Assembly be formed since the present one had failed in its task of fashioning a constitution *for* India. Several others, while not as extreme in their condemnation, were deeply disappointed that instead of a new, ideal constitution, what was presented was an intelligently framed copy.

There was much anguish that the village, long considered the beating heart of the Indian nation, did not even find mention in the Constitution. Even as Ambedkar set about adapting provisions of the Constitution from elsewhere in the world, he and the rest of the Drafting Committee members did not consider forms of local government and constitutional thinking in ancient and medieval India. Members brought to the notice of the house the work of Sri Aurobindo where he had outlined the centrality of the village community to the Indian way of life. Radha Kumud Mookerji had painstakingly documented the nature of local government in ancient India – constitutional thinking that pre-dated the American and French constitutions by centuries.[29] This was an alternative way of thinking about governance: vest sovereign power at the local level, enable individuals to directly participate in government, and empower them to lift themselves up by the bootstraps to do good for themselves and their communities. Much work was needed to adapt such a decentralized model to the existing framework under the Government of India Act, of a large state with towering institutions and a heavily centralized machinery. Alternatively, the framework itself would have to be changed altogether. But no such work was even started because Ambedkar dismissed such fanciful ideas outright. For him, the village, which represented local government, was a 'sink of localism' that had given rise to narrow-mindedness and communalism. It had no place in a modern constitution. Ambedkar didn't just ignore traditional constitutional thinking in India – he actively abjured it.

So non-traditional was Ambedkar's way of thinking

about the Constitution that a member, Mohammad Tahir, remarked that people would think that 'though the Englishman has left India, his ghost is yet stalking the country'.[30] British imperialism had been cemented through the all-powerful viceroy in Delhi exercising sovereign power in India in the name of the king of England. The simplest antidote to such imperialism would have been to decentralize power, devolve it closer to the people. Why should the minimum support price for paddy be paid for by the Union government through an elaborate network of agents and intermediaries and not the local panchayat directly? Why should roads in a small town be funded by the government in the state capital and not be the responsibility of local corporators? These may appear commonsensical but there was a widely prevalent view that local elements were more likely to be corrupt, self-serving, and narrow-minded. Trusting them with sovereign power was out of the question. Even making them ready to exercise it by creating local-level representative institutions was not considered. For Ambedkar, progressivism meant taking government far away from venal, partisan local governments to enlightened national leaders. To ensure that such national leaders did not become self-aggrandizing, Ambedkar took a tried-and-tested route of dividing powers between elected and unelected persons.

Central to this vision was the Rajya Sabha, the upper house of Parliament. This house would comprise indirectly elected representatives of State Legislatures, nominated members, intellectuals, artists and veteran leaders. These wise men and women were expected to 'introduce an element of sobriety and second thought',[31] preventing the elected Lok Sabha from being carried away by the currents of the day. In the British set-up, the House of Lords was a way for minor royalty, rich landowners, and other storied representatives of the permafrost of the British aristocracy to continue to have a say in the future of a rapidly democratizing nation. The Government of India Act had imported the body, called it the Council of State, and filled it with representatives from the provinces in British India and princely states. Several members of the Constituent Assembly viewed this council as a 'dead weight upon the progress of the people'.[32] The Drafting Committee, however, assumed that with maharajas being replaced by representatives of democratic states and intellectuals, the Rajya Sabha would be critical in presenting the voice of the states at the federal level. Equally, it would hold 'dignified debate' and improve the quality of lawmaking.

For Tahir, this was a vestige of imperialism, of unelected, unrepresentative interests of the rich and powerful refusing to let go in newly independent and democratizing

India. N.G. Ranga, an economist from Oxford and future president of the free enterprise Swatantra Party, went further and said that the upper house would only put a 'special premium to conservatism'.[33] Noted freedom fighter Damodar Seth, accused in the 'Kakori conspiracy' of 1925 – the armed robbery of a train near Lucknow by members of the Hindustan Republican Association to fund its revolutionary activities[34] – paraphrased Harold Laski to put it plainly: 'the system of nomination is undemocratic, while that of indirect election maximises corruption.'[35]

Despite these fundamental objections, the discussion in the Constituent Assembly proceeded on the basis that the principle of the second chamber was accepted. Consequently, it focused on limiting the powers of the Rajya Sabha in relation to financial matters given its indirectly representative status, underlining its role in the procedure relating to impeachment of judges, and providing for joint sittings in case of disagreement between the two houses. Though some members continued to question the suitability of bicameralism for India,[36] the only formal amendment moved to do away with the second chamber was roundly unsuccessful.[37] The Rajya Sabha remained in the Constitution of India because, despite popular misgivings, it was tried and tested in other countries as a means of preventing democracy getting out of hand. This was the template of cautious copying that the rest of the Constitution would follow.

This is how the framers of the Constitution of India repurposed the Government of India Act to suit the needs of an independent nation. They looked at India much like the colonists did, albeit with radically different intentions. The people were not ready for democracy and had to be controlled – hence a long, detail-oriented constitution. The length of the Constitution had much to do with the fact that it reproduced large parts of the Government of India Act, itself a 326-page document with 321 provisions and 10 schedules. It was equally the product of the understanding that when people cannot be trusted to do the right thing, the Constitution has to make elaborate prescriptions. The framers of the Constitution were right in their assessment that Indians had not experienced modern democracy before and would have to be led to it gently. But somewhere along the way, gentle guidance became enlightened diktat. Only a constitution that does not trust its own people has to lay down banal prescriptions like fundamental duties to promote harmony and make citizens respect the national flag; one that does not trust the state has to exhort it to share resources for the common good and prevent monopolies; and one that does not trust its legislators has to lay down in excruciating detail what rules of procedure they must adopt. The Constitution was not designed to guide people towards true democracy; it was devised more as a holy book following which the people would get there.

The Union and state governments would be the *sutradhars* of the Constitution, disseminating its contents to the citizenry. This is why the Constitution created powerful governments, much like the colonists had done. However, unlike the colonists, governments in independent India were democratically elected and expressly mandated to protect the fundamental rights of citizens and create a welfare state. In this sense, it was neither a break from the past nor was it a blind perpetuation. It was a case of cautious copying to create a constitution that would be acceptable to all. In 1950, the only document that could generate such consensus was a tried-and-tested colonial one. The framers hoped that now that these colonial institutions would be run by Indians, they would be run for Indians.

In 1833, Thomas Macaulay had said in the House of Commons:

> It may be that . . . having become instructed in European knowledge, they [Indians] may, in some future age, demand European institutions. Whenever it comes, it will be the proudest day in English history. To have found a great people sunk in the lowest depths of slavery and

> superstition, to have so ruled them as to have made them desirous and capable of all the privileges of citizens, would indeed be a title to glory all our own.[38]

On 26 January 1950, as Indians celebrated the dawn of the republic with a new constitution, Macaulay would have been proud that Indians had, on their own, perpetuated, supported, and legislated for themselves a raft of colonial institutions to guide their journey as an independent nation. Ustad Mangu, still penniless, may not have shared his pride.

TWO

The Everything State

The framers believed that a big, empowered state that towered over the citizen would deliver progress. With the Directive Principles of State Policy, the state was nudged towards controlling the economy for the public good. Side by side, the police were given vast powers to ensure that no citizen posed a threat to law and order.

In the heady years following the end of the Second World War and before Indian independence, social and economic rights of individuals dominated global human rights conversations. President Roosevelt's Four Freedoms – freedom of speech, of worship, from want and from fear – integrated both classic civil and political rights and social and economic rights for the first time. The Soviet Constitution had a clear focus on economic rights of the proletariat, on which the country's freedom was founded. The Universal Declaration of Human Rights 1948 by the United Nations was the culmination of this trend of theoretical thought that saw social rights, traditionally considered unenforceable, now made an inseparable part of the inalienable human rights of individuals.

These global developments inevitably impacted the thinking of the framers of the Constitution of India. Specifically, there had always been a clear line of thought that freedom would not be meaningful if people went to sleep hungry. It would have to be the duty of the state to provide the basic requirements of life. But Western constitutions till then had largely steered clear of such tenets of economic democracy. The traditional thinking had always been that a country's constitution provides the political structure of government that would allow citizens to thrive and flourish. But the Constitution of India had the benefit of hindsight on how older constitutions had operated. B.N. Rau, the constitutional adviser, during his extensive travels abroad realized that a postcolonial constitution like India's could not simply replicate a Western stereotype. It would have to adapt such models to suit the needs of an aspiring constitutional democracy. Bold, original thinking was the need of the hour to decolonize the Constitution.

A Bold Idea and Its Dilution

In an early note in September 1946, even before the Constituent Assembly had been first summoned, Rau distilled his understanding of fundamental rights in constitutions around the world. There were two classes of rights in most constitutions: those which are capable of enforcement in courts of law and those which aren't. The latter, called 'fundamental rights' in the USSR Constitution and the erstwhile Weimar Constitution, were rights such as the right to work which required the state to positively take action and provide work.[1] They were quite unlike the right to free speech or the right to personal liberty which the state merely had to recognize and respect. Taking note of this distinction, the Irish Constitution called these principles 'directive principles of social policy'.[2] The influential Cambridge academic Dr Hersch Lauterpacht in his seminal International Bill of the Rights of Man also separated these two classes of rights.

Drawing from this concept of rights that aren't judicially enforceable, Rau initially formulated seven directive principles which were meant for the 'general guidance' of legislatures and governments.[3] The principles themselves were of eclectic origin: one, relating to maintenance of appropriate nutritional standards, was from the Food and Agriculture Organization, another relating to prohibition of child labour was from the Irish Constitution, basic rights to education, work, rest, and maintenance in old age were derived from the USSR Constitution, one pertaining to promotion of international peace and security was from the Havana Declaration of 1939, made at a working-class gathering held in Havana. Clauses that obligated the state to preserve India's linguistic diversity, promote weaker sections including Scheduled Castes and native tribes, and prevent communal discord were Rau's original additions.

In both concept and content, the directive principles

were shaped by Rau's belief that progress in independent India would be powered by a big state machinery. Private industry and civil society, albeit critical components of the new nation state, were never seen as foundations on which the nation would be built. Though active control of private industry through the new licence raj regime would come later, the Constitution itself was imbued with the idea that if India had to develop economically, the state needed not only to protect its citizens from harm but also to provide the basic necessities of life. As a result, the elaborate machinery of the colonial state – from the collector to the governor-general – would not be dispensed with. Rather, it would now be repeopled by Indians from top to bottom and repurposed to serve the greater common good.

Directive principles were central to this repurposing. It would now be the duty of the state to direct its resources to ameliorating the economic travails of Indians, providing citizens with a decent quality of life in a way the colonial state had never done. The independent Indian state, like its colonial predecessor, would continue to be a *mai-baap* sarkar, just not one run by *gora* sahibs. Though this has come to be accepted wisdom today, in 1950 it was a conscious choice made by Rau. In his travels abroad, Rau had found support for the proposition that the Constitution should privilege general welfare over individual rights both from Irish leader Eamon de Valera and a highly well-regarded American judge, Justice Learned Hand. General welfare would only ensue when the state was constitutionally empowered and mandated to take measures to promote the common good. In some preliminary notes on fundamental rights written in September 1946 in anticipation of the convening of the Constituent Assembly, Rau proposed that the state would provide the right to maintenance in old age, raise the level of nutrition, and ensure children were not employed in occupations unsuited to their age or strength.[4] Thus, contrary to the widely accepted liberal understanding that non-intervention by the state would mean the perpetuation of liberty, Rau proposed the opposite: liberty would only be meaningful when the state actively intervened to secure a decent life for all.

This fundamental view found its constitutional refuge in the Irish Constitution which had similar principles that required the state to provide for its citizens. It was understood in Ireland that these principles, though fundamental, could not be enforced through courts.[5] After all, courts of law could not order the state to provide an 'adequate occupation' to each citizen or protect 'orphans and the aged' without first assessing whether indeed this was feasible. Two principles came together as a result: first, that these directives were fundamental to governance; second, that they were unenforceable in courts.

Ambedkar supported this by saying that such principles were necessary to make India an economic democracy. His basic claim was that the strategy of democratic countries to entrust legislatures with the task of preventing the growth of powerful economic monopolies had failed. Since legislatures worked on adult suffrage, they were inevitably controlled by the rich and powerful. The history of democracy in the United Kingdom and the United States had shown that the influence of legacy interests and monetary might on politics was strong, despite free and fair elections. As a result, economic restraints on the powerful were scarcely legislated. Consequently, when faced with the stark choice of employment without rights or unemployment with full rights to speech and expression, it was inevitable, Ambedkar said, that 'the fear of starvation, the fear of losing a house, the fear of losing savings, if any, the fear of being compelled to take children away from school, the fear of having to be a burden on public charity, the fear of having to be burned or buried at public cost are facts too strong to permit a man to stand out for his fundamental rights'.[6] Seen in this way, the need to provide a decent quality of life was central to the constitutional project of safeguarding the liberty of the citizen. This was heady, original, post-war constitution making, charting a different course from Anglo-American constitutions and their single-minded focus on the political structure of government.

K.T. Shah, Ambedkar's fellow traveller in creating a large welfare state, took it further. He thought it a folly to consider civil and political rights as enforceable on the ground that they did not require the state to act. Any right to personal liberty would require the state to set up courts and tribunals as well as enact criminal and civil codes. Further, a right to free speech would require the police, as otherwise some would exercise their rights in a way that would prevent others from doing so. It was fallacious to assume that only social and economic rights such as the right to food or work required positive state action; civil and political rights required them as well; it was just that conventional wisdom had equated such action with the duties of the state in the first place. Shah's argument was simple: the duties of the state to provide work, food, and shelter should be made fundamental and enforceable.[7]

Through their interventions, Ambedkar and Shah took Rau's framework further and questioned the very distinction between enforceable fundamental rights and non-enforceable directive principles. While discussions around economic rights were not new – several members in the Constituent Assembly made repeated references to the Soviet Constitution where they were included and enforceable – they were certainly not widely heard of in Western constitutions from which most of the framers' wisdom was received. It was also unthinkable that the Government of India Act, 1935, or its predecessors would have provisions that would obligate the state to secure a healthy and productive life for Indians. Calling for principles in the Constitution to make India an economic democracy was certainly bold and original, especially since economic circumstances in India at the time were markedly poorer compared to the countries in the West whose constitutions served as models for the framers.

Such boldness, however, was tempered by the crucial fact that there was no debate whatsoever on making such directive principles binding. Despite Shah's strong theoretical objections that the fact of the state having to provide for economic rights of citizens should not be a ground to exclude them as enforceable rights, there was scarcely any serious discussion in the Drafting Committee or in the Assembly on the need to make them enforceable. It was conceded, very early on, that courts could not enforce such rights since they were beyond a judge's competence. If they were to be rights, then the breach of such rights would require methods of enforcement other than going to a court of law.

Surprisingly, neither Ambedkar nor Rau nor Shah

dwelt long on how these rights would be enforced. Ambedkar had placed these principles alongside other principles that would make India socialist. These included collective farms with common ownership, key industries being owned by the state, state monopoly over insurance, and other similar mandates that called for active provision by the state in every critical element of an individual's economic well-being. Taken together, these provisions were included in the article that dealt with remedies against invasion of fundamental rights. This was consistent with Ambedkar and Shah's theoretical framing that 'the right to free election without a full belly would be a mockery'.[8] Accordingly, state socialism and the organization of the economic structure of society would be necessary as a remedy to ensure that the exercise of a vote remained intact. But what if the directive principles themselves were not adhered to? This was a possibility that was considered but never seriously debated.

Shah warned the Sub-Committee on Fundamental Rights – one of the several committees appointed by the Constituent Assembly – that without making such provisions enforceable like all other rights, they would amount to 'window dressing without any stock behind that dressing'. They should not be seen merely as pedantic 'directives' but as central to life in the new nation. Every governmental authority should be placed under a firm duty to enforce them. Though the non-enforcement of such rights would not ordinarily be taken to court, this did not mean that two distinct categories of rights should be created. In a view well ahead of his time, Shah stated that the principles of social policy should be 'categoric injunctions . . . to be given effect to as soon as possible'.[9] Governments would have to provide for them as a mandate of the Constitution; otherwise the Constitution itself would be devoid of meaning.

Rajkumari Amrit Kaur and Hansa Mehta echoed this sentiment in a dissent note stating specifically that the provision of a Uniform Civil Code should not be a directive principle as it is 'vital to social progress'.[10] The Union must be placed under an obligation to enact it within five to ten years. The upshot of their intervention was that the distinction between justiciable fundamental rights that one could go to court to enforce and non-justiciable principles of social policy should be revisited. Justiciability, after all, was only a question of perception. It seemed for a moment as if lawyerly conservatism was being cast aside in favour of first-order needs.

The strength of these interventions did ensure that fundamental rights and directive principles were not kept in watertight categories with distinct nomenclatures.[11] But what transpired was not a recognition that directive principles could be enforced in court like fundamental rights. Instead, in a clever lawyerly formulation, the Advisory Committee on Fundamental Rights, headed by Sardar Patel, made both sets of provisions components of the same fundamental rights chapter, albeit in different parts. Part I rights were fundamental and enforceable by courts; Part II rights were principles of social policy fundamental to the governance of the country.[12] This was an optical gloss over what was a substantive dilution from Rau's draft and Ambedkar and Shah's suggestions. Rau had initially called for directive principles to override fundamental rights. Ambedkar and Shah had asked for both sets of provisions to be equally important. But while they were placed in the same chapter for optics, in substance, the radicalism of the argument was gone.

Legal-technical arguments had won the day in determining the future trajectory of directive principles. But the fluidity of the distinction between fundamental rights and directive principles became clear in the discussions in the Advisory Committee on Fundamental Rights, Minorities and Tribal and Excluded Areas. The right to equality ('all persons within the Union shall be equal before the law'[13]), a cornerstone of the fundamental rights chapter, had been taken out by the Sub-Committee on Fundamental Rights since it was felt that a court of law could not enforce it. But so absurd was the tenor of this recommendation that in a dissent note,

K.M. Munshi said that equality was 'a fundamental principle of jurisprudence in a democratic constitution';[14] that alone should give it a place in the fundamental rights chapter. Fundamental rights could not only be about enforcement; first and foremost, they had to be about the centrality of such values in the lives of citizens in independent India.

This principle, however, was applied inconsistently. The sub-committee had recommended the right to free and primary education for children below the age of fourteen as a fundamental right to be provided by the state within ten years of the commencement of the Constitution. This was deleted by the advisory committee on the ground that the provision could not be enforced and should instead find place in the directive principles chapter.[15] Underlying these inconsistently executed swaps between enforceable rights and non-enforceable principles was an unspoken understanding that fundamental rights were the provisions that truly mattered. K.M. Panikkar didn't even comment on the directive principles 'as they create no legal rights'.[16] The advisory committee itself did not hold a full discussion on these principles; their interim report did not even contain a reference to these principles. It was only in a short supplementary report that the non-enforceable rights, by now renamed 'Fundamental Principles of Governance', made an appearance.[17] These principles, despite their grand title, were on their way to becoming footnotes to the fundamental rights chapter.

To prevent this from happening, a valiant attempt was made by the person who had originally suggested the incorporation of these principles: B.N. Rau. He said that if a municipality had to demolish unhealthy slums in the interest of public health, it would be unable to do so as such action would violate the right to property of the slum owners. In his full draft Constitution, he specifically asked the Drafting Committee to consider a clause that would not invalidate a law such as this only because it was contrary to fundamental rights.[18] Simply put, he wanted to reverse the hierarchy: directive principles would in effect be superior to fundamental rights.[19]

But the lawyer-dominated Drafting Committee, despite being led by Ambedkar, did not incorporate this radical change in the draft Constitution it presented to the Assembly in February 1948. It tinkered with the wording on the enforceability of the principles, omitting the words that it would be 'for the guidance of the state'.[20] Instead, it replaced 'guidance' with the strong term 'duty' and said that the state would now have a duty to apply these principles in making laws. But would the state abide by this duty because the Constitution said so or would a punitive mechanism be required? What if it simply did not provide free education and healthcare because it was too expensive to do so? The Drafting Committee remained conspicuously silent on these possibilities.

Ambedkar's rousing rhetoric in March 1947 arguing for state socialism now appeared fanciful, merely a year later. When the opportunity arose to make the collective good superior to individual entitlement, he demurred. At once a trained lawyer, a rights-first liberal, an anti-caste crusader, and a strident critic of Brahminical society, Ambedkar made his peace with the dilutions in the directive principles chapter. From the sub-committee and the advisory committee, it was evident that the principles themselves had started their long slide down from fundamental rights to lofty declarations. This presented Ambedkar the draftsman with an opportunity to accommodate diverse viewpoints that could not find place in other parts of the Constitution. Directives to create a socialist state could now harmlessly be added to the Constitution in a non-binding chapter. The radicalism of a constitution that promised economic democracy over political democracy, privileged the general good of the community over individual entitlement, was cut to size. Conventional wisdom prevailed: the Constitution now gave Indians the rights to speak, assemble, and trade, but not the entitlement to have their stomachs full, nor a roof over their heads, nor a school for their children. These promises would now be in a self-contained directive principles chapter. The chapter itself would be a convenient receptacle of accommodation, a veritable 'dust-bin of sentiment',[21] full of rhetoric, signifying plenty but entailing nothing.

A Dustbin of Sentiment

Primed for inclusion in the directive principles chapter were Gandhian principles of government that had failed to make any credible dent elsewhere in the constitutional text. Gandhi's radical promise to upend Western-style constitutional democracy and replace it with village-led, bottom-up governance with strict duties for citizen and state had many admirers in the Assembly. This had the makings of an alternative vision of India which was founded on and focused on its villages. The panchayat of five men and women from the village would be the 'legislature, judiciary and executive combined'.[22] Villages would be self-contained units, self-sufficient wherever possible, with the panchayat to ensure resolution of difficulties and conflicts. Economic progress would not be based on the industrial state but rather a self-sufficient agrarian economy. While Gandhi had not fully worked out the economic justifications for this alternative worldview, as a matter of principle, it resonated widely with the members of the Assembly.

But before the Assembly had a chance to fully consider what ought to be included or not in the Constitution, the Drafting Committee had already circulated a full draft in February 1948. Aside from its specific details, the template on which the draft was based was a tried-and-tested one: it provided for the major organs of government, rights of individuals, citizenship provisions, and ancillary provisions relating to amendments and transitions. With the exception of the removal of untouchability that had been made an article of faith in the fundamental rights chapter, other specific Gandhian mandates like enforcement of prohibition and instituting village democratic units were absent. Since a chapter on directive principles such as the right to work and education was also included, this chapter provided an ideal opportunity to include several Gandhian principles, without real consequences.

Mahavir Tyagi set the tone for discussions in the Assembly on prohibition. He candidly stated, 'I see nothing Gandhian in this Constitution . . . Gandhi had always been keen on total prohibition in the country, but the Constitution does not say a word about it.'[23] Inclusion of prohibition became almost a sine qua non if the framers were to remain true to the spirit of Gandhian politics. Jaipal Singh, a representative of the Scheduled Tribes, however, strongly contested its inclusion, pointing out how imbibing alcohol was part of some traditional ways of life.[24] Another member, B.H. Khardekar from Kolhapur, questioned the economic rationale of prohibition. He urged taxing of alcohol and using the revenue to build the country's educational and health indices rather than ban the consumption of alcohol altogether.[25]

Ambedkar deftly sidestepped both objections. He took recourse to what would become a standard argument: prohibition, while significant, was only a directive principle. Every state did not have to pass a law of this nature, and if they did, tribal councils – self-governing institutions for tribal areas – could override them in their specific context. This unique feature – the ability to accept prohibition while at the same time not accepting it – was the genius of the directive principles chapter as well as the seed of its own irrelevance.

This dissonance sharply emerged with an amendment proposed by K. Santhanam, a renowned newspaper editor and the railway minister in Nehru's first cabinet, to enable village panchayats to function as units of self-government. This amendment, which captured the essence of several speeches before it, was based on the principle that 'the entire structure of self-government, of independence in this country should be based on organised village community life'.[26] This principle had the potential of upending the Westminster form of government – with a legislature, executive, and judiciary both at the Union level and in every state – that is today taken for granted as essential to all government. In this alternative vision, government would mean small groups of elders in the village who would decide what is best for their own communities. Community life would take precedence over individual entitlements which would be part of a larger whole. The country would be built bottom-up, on the backs of millions of such self-governing villages flowering in their own ways. What exactly would happen to town and city government was not entirely clear.

This amendment was widely supported in the Assembly. In fact, T. Prakasam, who later became the first chief minister of the state of Andhra Pradesh, lamented that had the members got their act together earlier, this principle would have been the cornerstone of the entire Constitution. Prakasam was referring to the fact that most members had other important political work. He himself was involved in demanding the reorganization of states along linguistic lines, a matter that took up a lot of political time. During this time, B.N. Rau and the Drafting Committee had soldiered on in the work of creating and circulating a full draft to the Assembly. Though it was now too late to reorient the Constitution to Gandhian thinking, Santhanam's amendment provided a compromise that would be true to both Gandhi and the genius of traditional village life in India.

It was precisely such traditional village life that Ambedkar had described as the 'ruination of India'. He expressed happiness that the Constitution 'discarded the village and adopted the individual as its unit'.[27] For him, the village was the playground for caste Hindus who treated untouchables as less than human. While the question of individual rights was a far cry, Dalits were disallowed from entering temples and drawing water from wells, and often had to sweep the dust left by their feet off the ground through a trailing broom in an act of awful humiliation. Any reversion to self-governing villages, for Ambedkar, meant a return to this ignominious existence for millions of persons, like himself, belonging to lower castes. Such a vision had to be wholly rejected. A modern constitution based on fundamental rights of individuals, a large state invested with the express constitutional duty of respecting such rights and delivering welfare to citizens, and an independent judiciary to adjudicate these rights was the way forward for modern, democratic India.

But now, in the middle of 1948, in the shadow of Gandhi's assassination, with member after member invoking his memory, Ambedkar, without explanation, accepted Santhanam's amendment. This was an ideological contradiction of immense proportions: Ambedkar had categorically stated that the individual citizen was the focus of the Constitution, rights were invested in them, and the state was responsible for their fulfilment. The village unit had not figured. Here was a principle that stated otherwise, yet he concurred.

Ambedkar, the draftsman, was content with any inconsonant principles as long as they were included in the chapter on directive principles. He was aware of the contradiction of a top-down federal form of government that gave no legislative or executive powers to local governments now providing space for village units to operate within the framework. But he went along with this incorporation because the directive principles were not binding, but only a recognition of where the country wanted to go. Optimal compromises were after all a draftsman's stock-in-trade.

But the directive principles presented a far more fundamental compromise of constitutional ideology. This became most evident in the chapter's incorporation of principles of state socialism. Ambedkar had gone so far as to suggest that these principles themselves would be the remedy for violation of fundamental rights. This meant that every individual could claim in court, when they had been discriminated by their employer, that the state was duty-bound to take over that industry and ensure equal treatment of all workers. In this way, a socialist state would assure the liberty of citizens by working for the common good. Despite their critical importance, Ambedkar agreed to the downgrading of features of a socialist state as mere non-enforceable directive principles. No one could go to court claiming a violation, let alone asking the state to take over any industry to compensate for a wrong done.

Many of the principles that made it to the chapter were so watered down that many members sharply commented on their meaninglessness. Shibban Lal Saksena strongly argued for the need to ensure that all key industries were with the state, which was an article of faith of the Congress party. Jabudana Sahaya expressed a similar sentiment, rather more bluntly:

> You have here magnificent and sparkling words, social justice, political justice and economic justice. Very good and splendid words but they appear very far away from the toiling millions. Why not state here, not today, not tomorrow but in the distant future that the community will own what belongs to the community by the gift of nature and by the gift of God.[28]

Despite the dissent, the Constitution provided for neither state ownership of industries nor community rights. Ambedkar the lawyer knew that any such provisions would squarely contradict the right to property, which had been recommended by the Advisory Committee headed by Sardar Patel as a fundamental right. The sheer brilliance of his earlier speech arguing for economic democracy to be constitutionally provided for paled now before his pragmatism in settling for an aspiration for socialism in the Constitution. The directive principles provided a convenient receptacle to facilitate such fundamental compromises on ideology.

First Rau and later Ambedkar had envisaged the repurposing of the big colonial state to serve the economic interest of citizens. But no sooner had this ideological repurposing taken place than its radical potential was blunted through conservative legal drafting. Instead of a truly original constitution, laying down in categorical terms how the economy was to be organized, what remained, as reflected in the directive principles chapter, was a big state with a set of aspirations which the framers hoped it would one day realize.

Had any of these principles been mandated, the Constitution would have taken a major step towards becoming truly transformative and original. But straitjacketing these principles into a chapter that could not be enforced meant that their originality and promise both remained stillborn. They nudged India towards a socialist state without mandating it, promised economic democracy without guaranteeing it, laid down a destination of a fair, just, and equal society without the path that would get society there. As T.T. Krishnamachari remarked, the directive principles were 'sufficiently resilient as to permit any individual of this House to ride his hobby horse into it'.[29] Though he was being sarcastic, the framers certainly used this opportunity to cram in every Gandhian principle that had been left out of other parts of the Constitution.

As a result, the chapter had something for everyone – its backers had the satisfaction that a value they cherished had found place in the Constitution, its detractors derived comfort that none of it would ordinarily be enforced. This was its true genius: that, despite being part of the Constitution, the supreme law, it left what was to become of the principles to the wisdom of succeeding generations. The chapter's structure was borrowed from Ireland but appropriated fully with values that the framers believed were central to the Constitution of the new Indian nation. Yet these values themselves, pillars of a socialist state, were not taken to their logical conclusion and mandated as binding principles. As a result, the repurposing of the big, colonial state remained incomplete. The state remained large and present in all spheres of economic activity, contrary to what Gandhi had imagined, yet not fully set on the path of radical economic change. Lawyerly conservatism had prevailed over socialist ideology and Gandhian philosophy. The big law and order state could stay, but both the big socialist state and the self-sufficient Gandhian village unit had to wait their turn.

A Police Constable's Constitution

'Let me put it a little more strongly. I feel that many of these fundamental rights have been framed from the point of view of a police constable.'[30] Somnath Lahiri may have been the only member of the Constituent Assembly who was a card-carrying member of the Communist Party of India, but his objection to how the fundamental rights chapter had been drafted wasn't merely ideological – it was factual.

Fundamental rights of citizens were to be the crown jewel of the new constitutional framework. Accordingly, the sub-committee tasked with the job of formulating these rights comprised a galaxy of legal stalwarts, Alladi Krishnaswamy Ayyar and B.R. Ambedkar, noted public intellectuals, Maulana Abul Kalam Azad, Acharya Kripalani, and Minoo Masani, besides several other leading lights of the freedom movement. They were vested with the critical task of incorporating the spirit of the freedom struggle in a well-defined chapter of the Constitution.

That spirit was epitomized by the Declaration of Purna Swaraj by the Congress in 1930.[31] At a time when human rights for all Indians were a far cry, the Congress had resolved that 'it is the inalienable right of the Indian people, as of any other people, to have freedom and to enjoy the fruits of their toil and have the necessities of life, so that they may have full opportunities of growth'.[32] Embedded within this statement were the four kinds of freedom that the struggle for freedom envisioned: political, with freedom of speech and expression; cultural, with an education system freed from colonial moorings that does not 'hug the very chains that bind us'; spiritual, to look inward and channelize that inner strength into self-protection; and economic, to be self-sufficient and freed from the cesspool of exploitation that characterized colonial rule. The Karachi Resolution of 1931 on fundamental rights and economic freedoms even concretized these concepts into constitutional form with a list of rights to be enjoyed by every citizen.

When it came to drafting the actual Constitution of India, however, the sub-committee was far more cautious than when its individual members were advocating for freedom. Now that they had a government to think about administering, most of these rights of citizens and obligations of the state were no longer ideals. Though they were incorporated in some form, their edge was blunted through caveats and exceptions. This was consistent with how the Drafting Committee later went about its task of drafting the Constitution: it was to be a practical document capable of governing India, not a combined wish list of demands made during the freedom struggle. As a result, even core beliefs of the struggle, like the active advocacy of abolition of salt duty, were discarded. This is the most telling symbol of how the fundamentals of the freedom struggle were not the wellsprings from which the fundamental rights in the Constitution emanated.

While the march to Dandi to protest the imposition of a tax on salt was the most visible expression of Gandhi's anti-salt tax politics, his views against this 'barbarous practice' were long held.[33] During the time he was in South Africa, he closely followed developments relating to British policies on salt in India. When a rumour was floated that the salt tax would be abolished to commemorate the visit of the Prince of Wales in November 1905, Gandhi wrote, 'every Indian sincerely hopes that this is well founded and will prove true'.[34] Salt, like air and water, for him, was one of the necessities of life. Particularly on the west coast of India with its large salt pans, it was nature's bounty for humans to use responsibly. By regulating its production and imposing a heavy tax on its consumption (Gandhi stated that it was 3 per cent of the total tax collections of the colonial government, though that figure is doubtful), the colonial government became a 'Government that steals the people's salt and makes them pay heavily for the stolen article'.[35] For him, 'the people, when they become conscious of their power, will have every right to take possession of what belongs to them'.[36]

But when Indians became masters of their own constitutional fate and took sovereign control over the production and manufacture of salt, instead of abolishing the tax on salt, the Constituent Assembly chose pragmatically to continue it. In the draft Constitution prepared by the Drafting Committee, draft Article 253 had initially stated, 'No duties on salt shall be levied by the Union.' But the matter wasn't as simple: the provision was qualified with an asterisk stating that the majority of the Drafting Committee were opposed to such a provision; it was only retained at the instance of Alladi Krishnaswamy Ayyar. For the others, questions relating to salt regulation were matters for Parliament and not the Constitution.[37]

This view was conceptually sound. Matters relating to regulation of specific items were not ordinarily the subject matter of any constitution. But salt was not just another item: it was arguably the most visible symbol of the freedom struggle. For a constitution that otherwise paid little importance to brevity including within it inordinate details of procedures to be followed in Parliament and State Legislatures – how expenses of public service commissions would be charged, how interstate river water disputes were to be adjudicated, and in providing for grants in lieu of export duty on jute products to be paid by the Government of India to encourage jute export by states – to suddenly insist on leaving the matter of taxing salt to Parliament was curious. Biswanath Das called it 'a sentimental provision'[38] that only pandered to black marketers. Ambedkar pointed to the fact that a blanket prohibition would mean that the Union would not be able to levy customs duty on foreign salt as well, an entirely unintended consequence. Jawaharlal Nehru was sanguine in his belief that even without the prohibition, no government in India would tax salt. Stupefied on hearing these views, Rajendra Prasad, in an uncharacteristically frank expression of his personal beliefs as president of the Constituent Assembly, advised the committee to retain the prohibition 'as a memento of that glorious struggle which we had'.[39] But the ship had sailed. Naziruddin Ahmed summed it up succinctly: 'We have violated the sacred principles of Mahatma Gandhi so often in this Constitution that the deletion of clause (1) [prohibition of levy on salt] should not be objectionable on that account.'[40]

The Mahatma was dead, so irreverent statements of this nature were perhaps more easily tolerated. But even otherwise, for the drafters of the Constitution, a vast majority of whom were active participants in the freedom struggle, to disregard their own experiences and their sentiments while drafting the Constitution was an insight into how they perceived the nature of their task in the Constituent Assembly. Now that they were in the saddle, gone were their days of advocacy and campaigning. Instead, that desire for justice and fair play was channelized into creating a governmental machinery which, unlike its colonial predecessor, would work in the best interests of the people. This would only be possible if the widest possible latitude were to be given both to Parliament and to the executive government to act, untrammelled by excessive checks and balances. This was the core idea underpinning the colonial constitution – if India was to prosper, it needed a big state. Now that the state would be run by Indians, there was no need to fear overreach.

The clearest expression of this idea was in the fundamental rights chapter. Fundamental rights were guaranteed to every citizen of independent India, in a marked departure from colonial rule. All persons would have the right to life and personal liberty, to the freedom of religion, to equality before the law and equal protection of laws. Citizens would also have the right to free speech, to form associations, to assemble peacefully, to move and reside freely throughout the country, and to take up any profession, trade, or occupation. Critically, if any of these rights were denied, persons also had a fundamental right to approach the Supreme Court of India directly. This remedy was, in Ambedkar's words, the 'very heart' and the 'very soul' of the Constitution,[41] making fundamental rights real and enforceable.

But when could such rights be said to have been violated? Unlike the Declaration of the Rights of Man, which inspired these fundamental rights, the rights in the Indian Constitution were not lofty declarations, but bounded ones. Each right was countervailed by certain powers of the state to restrict those rights on specific grounds. Free speech could be restricted in the interests of the sovereignty and integrity of India, the right to free association could be circumscribed by the need for public order, and the right to life itself could be limited by the state acting according to the procedure established by law. All of these restrictions would have to be reasonable in nature and would have to be made by law.

There was nothing exceptional about restricting rights in certain situations. That my right to swing my fist ended where your nose began was a classical tenet of liberal theory. The Sub-Committee on Fundamental Rights, the Advisory Committee on Fundamental Rights, and then the Drafting Committee all considered it normal for rights to be restricted by the state. The question however was: how far could such restrictions extend? Alladi Krishnaswamy Ayyar gave his colleagues on the sub-committee the example of the US Constitution where the text itself was silent on restrictions and gave the impression that rights were absolute.[42] But restrictions came in over time through judgments of the US Supreme Court. Later constitutions had attempted to codify these restrictions in the text itself, an approach that the sub-committee appeared to favour. K.M. Munshi captured this well in his suggestion – a single article on 'Exemptions and Qualifications' that determined the extent to which rights could be restricted by Parliament or State Legislatures. Broadly speaking, the state would have an overriding power to restrict a fundamental right when there was a 'grave emergency'.[43]

This was commonsensical, but not to all members of the Assembly. Somnath Lahiri was baffled: 'Now, Sir, what constitutes a "grave emergency" God alone knows.'[44] Capacious terms such as 'grave emergency' would be given meaning by the government of the day. Part of this objection may have been semantic. After all, it is impossible to define an emergency exhaustively. That is why the drafters of the Constitution had kept the door open for any declaration of emergency to be challenged in the Supreme Court if it appeared to be a ruse.

But some part of this objection was substantive. There was a general sense in the Constituent Assembly that the state would be the guarantor of the liberty of citizens and not its transgressor. The idealism of establishing a new governmental machinery had infused the drafters of the Constitution with a spirit of trust and fellow feeling. Gone was Gandhi's admonishment that without curtailing the powers of the state, independent India may resemble 'Englistan': colonial rule supervised by Indian, instead of British, officers. Instead, Nehru's belief that Indians were now 'a nation which is full of the passion for freedom'[45] carried the day. That Indians were in charge of their own destiny meant that citizens would have to trust the state and vice versa; the previous relationship of servitude and overlordship was over.

This idealism was captured in the Objectives Resolution. The passage of this resolution by the Constituent Assembly in January 1947 was meant to provide a foundation for the drafting of the Constitution. The five pillars of the Objectives Resolution were sovereignty, independence, freedom, equality, and becoming an integral part of the post-war global order. It was a ringing declaration that the time had come for India to take its rightful place amongst the commonwealth of nation states and that it would do so responsibly.

As a declaration of intent, it was certainly stirring. 'It is a Declaration. It is a firm resolve. It is a pledge and an undertaking and it is for all of us I hope a dedication,' said Jawaharlal Nehru, moving it in the Assembly.[46] He urged members not to see the declaration in terms of its 'narrow legal wording'[47] but the spirit that animated it. But what was that spirit? At a fundamental level, it was the spirit of renaissance, of a suppressed nation reverting to its rightful position on the global stage.

Equally, it epitomized the spirit of pragmatism. For a resolution that claimed as its inspiration the Tennis Court Oath of Paris in 1789, when the members of the third estate comprising ordinary French citizens took an oath as the self-appointed 'National Assembly' to draft a constitution for France, the constitutional convention in the United States to draft the US Constitution, and the more recent Russian Revolution, it was quick to declare that all freedoms were subject to law and public morality. This was a critical qualification to demonstrate that the drafting of the Constitution was not simply an ideological exercise. It was a practical document that was being created to fashion a government out of a movement, a nation out of a people. To function, governments needed powers and an excessive emphasis on fundamental rights of individuals was antithetical to such power. Even in a declaration, this pragmatic element – of inalienable rights coexisting with far-reaching governmental powers and responsibilities – remained unmistakably clear.

The starkest expression of the need to establish the state as a guarantor of liberty, as opposed to its chief threat, came in the provisions on preventive detention in the chapter on fundamental rights. Preventive detention laws had been a weapon of choice of the colonial administration in dealing with Indian freedom fighters. Most notably, the Rowlatt Act, officially titled the Anarchical and Revolutionary Crimes Act, 1919, authorized police to detain persons without trial, try without a jury, and search without a warrant. It was pointedly directed at diluting the protections afforded by the Code of Criminal Procedure to freedom fighters who had been accused of crimes against the British government.[48] Gandhi had termed it a 'black act',[49] a law 'of such a character that no self-respecting nation can accept it'.[50] So when the time came that Indians were in charge of their own destiny and could rewrite all colonial laws, one might be forgiven for thinking that preventive detention, the signature symbol of the lawlessness of the British Raj, would be consigned to the dustbin of history.

Instead, the founding fathers hedged their bets. The Drafting Committee by a vote of 2:1 took the pragmatic step of incorporating safeguards regarding the use of preventive detention into the Constitution itself. This gave rise to the remarkable situation that a chapter on fundamental rights of citizens dedicated a long provision to the power of the state to preventively detain them. Ambedkar, to the surprise of many, was the swing vote in securing the legal safety of preventive detention.

In one stroke, the Constitution not only legitimized preventive detention but also signalled that in newly democratic India, the needs of security of the state were weightier than the new-found freedom of citizens. There was certainly some justification for this view. Ambedkar, who was fundamentally responsible for conceptualizing the preventive detention provision and steering it through the Assembly, repeatedly pointed to the need for a strong state in dealing with the 'present circumstances in the country',[51] the violence in the aftermath of Partition, and uprisings in several parts of the country. Several sittings of the Assembly were disrupted as a result of riots and curfews, members were issued special passes to enable them to attend the sessions, and Muslim members were given additional armed protection.[52] In this backdrop, Ambedkar was able to reject the amendments proposed by the 'enthusiasts for personal liberty' in the Assembly. Pragmatism trumped principle and the values of the freedom movement were given short shrift.

For Ambedkar, draft Article 15A legitimizing preventive detention (later renumbered Article 22 of the Constitution of India) was critical to ensure that citizens were not jailed arbitrarily.[53] It was laid out in the form of a series of safeguards ensuring that individuals who were detained were informed of the reasons for their detention, allowed to consult with a lawyer of their choosing, kept confined only for a limited period, which could only be extended with the authorization of an impartial advisory board. But these safeguards could not mask the fundamental upshot of the provision itself: in principle, preventive detention was permissible in India's constitutional framework.

Not only was the Drafting Committee cognizant of the possibility of abuse of preventive detention powers, but it was also aware of the likelihood of such abuse being high. This is because the Drafting Committee had decided to delete the words 'due process of law', instead choosing the more benign 'procedure established by law' in the provision on the fundamental right to life and personal liberty. This meant that a person could be detained as long as a law which provided for preventive detention prescribed a clear procedure – the more onerous 'due process' requirement that such a law had to be fair, just, and reasonable would not have to be met.[54] More detentions were quite likely as a result of this change.

Of course, the reason this change had been made was distinct. The constitutional adviser B.N. Rau had been advised by Justice Frankfurter of the US Supreme Court that the 'due process' clause in the US Constitution had meant that courts had the authority to strike down a range of social welfare legislation. There was a real apprehension in the Constituent Assembly that a future programme of social revolution in independent India would be derailed by a strict Supreme Court that would interpret the right to personal liberty widely. At the same time, the mass violence that had erupted after Partition meant that the state would have to deal with riotous elements with a heavy hand. The drafters were careful that a constitutional guarantee of 'due process' should not be pressed into service of personal liberty of either rioters causing violence or ryotwaris who had accumulated large tracts of land and would stand in the way of redistribution.

To obviate this process, the 'due process' standard was deleted entirely. Ambedkar was cognizant that such a change would have a hugely damaging impact on the civil liberties of citizens. They would now not be able to challenge any law that allowed for long periods of detention without access to legal counsel or having to be presented before a magistrate. But he went along with this change. This led Mahavir Tyagi to remark snidely: 'Dr Ambedkar will please pardon me when I express my fond wish that he and the other members of the Drafting Committee had had the experience of detention in jails before they became members of the Drafting Committee.'[55]

There was more than a kernel of truth to this statement. Except for K.M. Munshi, the Drafting Committee appeared to consider the question of preventive detention an intellectual exercise in wordsmithing rather than an existential question of life and death. Their limited experience of personally having been jailed may have contributed to this view. But more importantly, the Drafting Committee genuinely believed that a big state in all respects could deliver security and prosperity for Indians. This is why, for the first time in a democratic constitution, the use of preventive detention laws even during peacetime was authorized, ostensibly with a view to providing some safeguards for detenus to make up for the loss of 'due process'. The feeling was that such detention would take place anyway as it would often be felt necessary for law and order. In anticipation of this, the framers felt it might be better to authorize and limit it, rather than turn a blind eye to it after legislating it out of existence. Even the British did not have such powers at home, such was the irony of this position taken by the newly independent republic of India. By privileging security over liberty, the state over the citizen, the framers were clear – though freedom was not won by the barrel of a gun, its continuance would certainly depend on one.

If more proof was needed, it came on 25 February 1950. The Constituent Assembly sitting as the provisional Parliament passed the Preventive Detention Act, 1950, authorizing police officers in the newly independent Union of India and its constituent states to detain its citizens on mere suspicion, for extended periods, without production before a magistrate or a trial.[56] Somnath Lahiri was right: the Constitution, or at least some parts of it, did look like it had been drafted by and for the police constable. The big colonial state was here to stay.

THREE

New Delhi Darbar

The Constitution created a federation with elected state governments responsible for local governance. But it created an even more powerful Union government in New Delhi that could dismiss state governments much like the colonial administrators could during the Raj.

When the Constituent Assembly met for the first time on 9 December 1946, the nation was gripped by the excitement of imminent independence. The Cabinet Mission had laid out its plan of setting up a Constituent Assembly to draft the Constitution for a free India. The Constituent Assembly was charged with a task that had been a principal demand of the Congress party for a decade. But when it gathered in the Central Hall of Parliament to fulfil this lofty purpose, the enormity of the moment was outstripped by the utter uncertainty of the nature of the exercise. Was it going to be a constitution for a united India? Was the Muslim League going to join the deliberations? Would the unity of India hold or would Pakistan soon become a reality? The overhang of a possible partition loomed large in the minds of the drafters.

As a consequence, that first meeting of the Assembly wasn't the joyous occasion one might have expected it to be. The mood in the Constitution Hall was solemn.

Its oldest member, Sachchidananda Sinha, reminded his colleagues that the establishment of the Constituent Assembly had been 'an article of faith' for the country for over a decade.[1] Now that the Assembly had been set up, its labours should be guided by 'a vision which may restore India to her pristine glory'.[2] But Sinha knew, as did his younger colleagues in the Assembly, that such restoration would not become reality with the Muslim League boycotting the proceedings.

Jinnah had been steadfast in his intention that a separate Constituent Assembly be set up for Pakistan. The firmness underlying this intention had somewhat thawed when the Cabinet Mission announced its intention of creating a single Constituent Assembly, albeit with three sections comprising Hindu-majority provinces, Muslim-majority provinces in the north-west, and a combination of Muslim majority Bengal and Hindu-majority Assam in the east respectively. Each section would draft its own constitution for its group of provinces, with only foreign affairs, defence, and communications left to the Union. This was a significant concession to the League's demands and largely fulfilled its aspirations of self-government for Indian Muslims. But when the Congress insisted that Punjab in Group 2 and Assam in Group 3 should be given the option to withdraw unilaterally from their groups, the Muslim League rejected the idea of a single Constituent

Assembly in totality.[3] Its seats in Parliament House in Delhi remained unfilled.

With the brinkmanship of the Muslim League, the prospect of an independent and sovereign Pakistan inched ever closer to reality. As the idea of Pakistan took concrete shape, uppermost on the minds of the framers of the Constitution was the need to preserve the territorial integrity of the rest of India. The risks of an insurgency or external aggression ultimately leading to secession of provinces from the Union, particularly those with distinct demographics or geographically at the margins, had to be firmly foreclosed. This needed a strong Union government, which, if push came to shove, could constitutionally overpower a recalcitrant state government into submission. The autonomy of each state would have to be curtailed, its finances would have to be tied to the Union and other states, and in case of an emergency that government itself should be capable of being suspended. For the framers, a model to achieve these purposes was readily available.

Rule, but Properly

Section 93 of the Government of India Act, 1935, allowed unelected governors to take over the administration of a province by proclaiming that an emergency had arisen. Such a proclamation could only be made with the concurrence of the governor-general in Delhi. It could be extended up to three years if the United Kingdom parliament authorized it. The governor-general could also, of his own accord, proclaim an emergency in a province, and authorize its direct governance from Delhi. In this manner, elected Indian legislators could be frozen out of provincial governments by unelected British overlords.

The history of this provision is as old as the history of popularly elected governments in colonial India. The Simon Commission in its report in 1930 had recommended 'responsible self-government' in provinces but was quick to add that the lynchpin of provincial governance would continue to be the unelected governors. Governors would be assisted in their task by a cabinet comprising a few elected ministers and other nominated persons, all of whom he could select. Even then, the Simon Commission felt it would be wise to further reserve powers at times of emergencies with the governor alone who could directly take over the entire reins of government. When government could not be carried out according to the law, presumably owing to riots, disturbances, insurrections, or an all-out revolt, the governor could take over all power, exclude his ministerial colleagues, and drop any pretence of democratic accountability. This, John Simon and his colleagues wrote, 'is no denial of self-government; it is the ultimate resource if self-government is repudiated'.[4]

This idea of emergency powers as a so-called safety valve for self-government was a recurrent theme in the British administration of India. The Joint Committee Report of 1934, which was a precursor to the Government of India Act, gave the unelected governor certain 'special responsibilities'.[5] These chiefly pertained to maintenance of law and order and protection of minorities. For such matters, the governor could override the provincial legislature and pass ordinances directly at any time.

Emergency powers expanded the same logic: if despite such unilateral ordinances (or because of them), peace was not restored and governance was impossible, the governor could vest all powers of administration in himself. Effectively this meant that the province would be administered by the unelected officers of the ICS, supervised by the unelected governor, answerable to the unelected governor-general and ultimately the unrepresentative UK parliament.

Such a situation arose with the resignation of the Congress ministries in 1939. Great Britain had declared war on Germany. It had made India a part of the war effort without as much as a token consultation with Indian leaders. Congress ministries in the United Provinces, Central Provinces, Bombay, Madras, Orissa, Bihar, and the North-West Frontier Province resigned in protest. In Punjab and Bengal, non-Congress coalition ministries comprising a combination of local parties, the Muslim League, and others formed the government.

With no elected government in power in seven provinces, Section 93 of the Government of India Act was invoked, which enabled the governor to take over all the functions of any provincial body or authority if he could satisfy himself that there was a 'failure of constitutional machinery' in the province. Using this power, the governors in several provinces became their de facto administrators. Simultaneously, the Government of India Act itself was amended to give the governor-general in Delhi executive power over provincial governments during the operation of an external emergency like war.

With a view to get Indian leaders onside in the war effort, Governor-General Linlithgow had said in a speech at the Orient Club in Bombay in 1940 that after the war India would be granted full dominion status.[6] This had failed to convince Congress leaders. For them, only a representative Constituent Assembly ought to decide India's constitutional fate. The Muslim League had a different view: by not outrightly condemning the British war effort, the League attempted to curry favour with the governor-general.

With the Congress and the League at loggerheads,

the UK parliament, while approving the proclamation of an emergency, urged communities to trust each other if India was to achieve self-rule.[7] Till such time, the British would continue to govern through Section 93 of the Government of India Act. This was the only way, the British parliamentarians felt, stable, impartial government could be offered to Indians at a time of political instability.

At a conceptual level, since someone had to run the government in the provinces, it was natural that the governor was given this responsibility. Equally importantly, for a colonial government that in any event conducted provincial affairs through the governor, dispensing with India's fledgling federal character and reverting to a unitary style of governance with a colonial governor, who was supervised by the governor-general, was a natural impulse. This is why no alternatives to wholesale handing over of power to the governor were even considered. There was always the default democratic option of holding fresh elections if possible or propping up a weakened provincial government from the outside with central forces, staff, and money till such time as any internal disturbance was quelled. But Governor's Rule suited colonial interests optimally and no alternatives were needed.

For the British, the power to proclaim an emergency was never really about a safety valve for self-government.

On the contrary, it neatly fitted into a fundamental belief of the superiority of the expert colonial administrator over the untrained Indian legislator. The question of representative government in India, according to Lord Macaulay, was 'utterly out of the question'.[8] Now, nearly a century later, this primitive belief found sophisticated expression in the governor's emergency powers. Leo Amery, secretary of state, summed it up pithily: 'This constitution [GOI Act, 1935] would allow Indians to rule the provinces as long as they do it *properly* [emphasis supplied], and leave the Governors absolutely free to take over the whole or any part of the administration themselves should the machine not function properly.'[9]

Indians could rule, but only if they could do it properly.

A Stupid Thing

One might be excused for believing that with the departure of the British such undemocratic sentiment would have departed too. But the growing intimacy between the Muslim League and the British, especially after the resignation of the Congress ministries, had chastened Congressmen in the Constituent Assembly and made them wary of secessionist tendencies, particularly at the frontiers of the nation. To offset this possibility, a strong Centre that could take over from state governments at a time of emergency was widely supported.[10] But the Cabinet Mission had recommended otherwise, creating a weak Union and strong provinces. The task of bridging these extreme positions was given to the Union Powers Committee of the Assembly.

Of the twelve members initially appointed to the committee by the president of the Assembly, Rajendra Prasad, eleven were lawyers by training or by profession. These included Nehru, Pant, Ayyangar, Ayyar, Khaitan, and Munshi.[11] Speaking on the need for this exercise, Rajagopalachari assured the Assembly that the committee would not undo the federal structure proposed in the Cabinet Mission Plan.[12] This was a diplomatic remark, intended to keep alive the possibility of the Muslim League participating in the Assembly.[13] In the two months that it was given to submit its report to the Assembly, the question before the committee was simple enough: 'whether there should be a strong Centre and if so what powers it should have.'[14] But the indecision surrounding the Muslim League's participation complicated things. It was as if the Pakistan question had cast a shadow over the committee's deliberations. Nehru, the chairman of the committee, articulated this difficulty in its first meeting: 'Though it was not yet clear, it was very probable that the Muslim League might keep out and, possibly, in the terms of the Cabinet Mission's Statement, they might have to be given a chance to come in too. They would have to wait a little more to come to final conclusions.'[15]

Given the fluidity of the situation, the first report of the committee was short, vague, and provided 'in general terms for a very weak Central Government'.[16] According to Ayyangar (himself a member of the committee), the report was altogether dissatisfactory, lacking precision and accuracy. The poor quality may be attributed to the fact that the committee did not have much time to put the report together. But the lack of precision and accuracy in the report was likely intentional. The committee was holding its horses until there was clarity on partition, the participation of the Muslim League in the Assembly, and the applicability of the Cabinet Mission Plan.

In June 1947, when Governor-General Mountbatten announced that within two months India and Pakistan would be partitioned into two separate nations, the Muslim League question became moot for the Constituent Assembly. The Union Powers Committee began holding joint sessions with the Union Constitution Committee, another Constituent Assembly committee set up to draft the provisions related to the Union government. The goal was clear: reintroduce a strong Union government into the Constitution. By this time, the Union Constitution Committee in its internal deliberations had already resolved that 'the Constitution should be a Federal structure with a strong Centre'.[17] On 21 July 1947, with Jinnah's explicit instruction to the Muslim League representatives to boycott all proceedings of the Assembly, immediate political considerations on the nature of the federation disappeared from the constitutional imagination. The Constituent Assembly would no longer have to adopt a delicate approach to the question of how strong the government at the centre would be vis-à-vis the states to placate the League. On the contrary, their experience of dealing with the Muslim League culminating in the partition of the country itself led to the principled belief that a united India required a strong Union. The first report of the Union Powers Committee had to be rejected.

By July, the second Union Powers Committee report was prepared. If the first report had been criticized for being too general and vague, the second report was terse, direct, and did not mince words. It attributed the weak Centre in the first report to the constraints imposed by the Cabinet Mission Plan and the shadow of the Muslim League. It undid such a framework and left no doubt in the minds of any member of the Constituent Assembly that an empowered Union was the way forward for India.

The conceptual foundation for an overwhelmingly strong Union was firmly in place by August 1947. In this light, it should not come as a surprise that despite Sections 93 and 102 of the Government of India Act on the powers of the unelected governor and governor-general being colonial vestiges, they were endorsed by members of the Constituent Assembly with great enthusiasm.[18] Foremost among their proponents was T.T. Krishnamachari, a leading intellectual from Madras and future finance minister of India. Echoing the safety valve theory, Krishnamachari opined that emergency powers were a 'necessary evil' to save the Constitution from being obliterated by forces antithetical to the nation. That the state would be clothed with unlimited powers and citizens would have no fundamental rights mattered very little. 'The free exercise of civil liberty – as it is called – God knows what it really means'[19] would not be abridged because parliamentary supervision would check any executive caprice. In any event, Krishnamachari believed that an emergency would be a situation so dire that the country would have to come together as one to combat it and suspension of the Constitution would be a wholly secondary matter. If it led to a 'constitutional dictatorship' with unlimited powers, so be it.

But Krishnamachari's rhetoric did not match the text of the constitutional provision. Specifically, the power to proclaim an emergency in the Constitution was not limited to the sorts of extreme situations that Krishnamachari had in mind. It could be proclaimed not just during a national emergency but even when there was an internal disturbance in some part of the country, either actual or imminent, or when a state government was unable to carry out its functions in accordance with the Constitution, in the view of the Centre. In fact, at the instance of the Drafting Committee led by Ambedkar, it was proposed that a disturbed state itself become a 'centrally administered area' with its democratically elected government being removed from office and the state assembly dissolved during the time the emergency was in effect.[20]

Dissenting members were startled by the severity of this sentiment, especially when it came to the provision of President's Rule in a state in the event that a state government could not function in accordance with the provisions of the Constitution. In such a situation, the president could dissolve the State Legislature and govern the state directly or through a delegate. During this time, the president would also have the power to suspend all fundamental rights including the right to move courts for redress.

For a constitution that proclaimed itself federal with division of sovereignty between the Union and states, both being supreme in their respective domains, the reversion to a unitary and unaccountable form of government during any disturbance in a state was unexpectedly quick. Kazi Karamuddin warned his compatriots in the Assembly of its consequences: 'No party which is in opposition to the Centre will be allowed to rule in a Province. That situation is bound to arise.'[21] H.V. Kamath, a thoughtful participant in debates on emergency provisions, surveyed every well-known constitution from which the framers had derived provisions to demonstrate that a sweeping provision of this nature did not exist in any of them. Even the British government during the Second World War did not suspend the right of persons to move courts of law during an emergency, as the Drafting Committee had recommended for the Constitution.[22] He put it simply and categorically: 'A general authorisation of this kind for restricting individual freedom has no parallel anywhere else.'[23]

Many concerned members spoke of the need for checks and balances on the power of the president to dissolve an elected legislature. The threshold – that government cannot be carried on in accordance with the Constitution – was too vague, there was no requirement of the president to consult anyone on the ground, including the governor, before such a radically undemocratic measure was taken. However, for the Drafting Committee and the majority of the Assembly, the conceptual antidote to any strife in the periphery of the country was to revert to a unitary form of government. As far as safeguards to prevent such a provision that signalled the death knell of federalism in

India, the Drafting Committee felt that vesting the power to proclaim emergency in the president who would act on the advice of his ministers, requiring periodic approval by Parliament for the continuance of an emergency, and setting a firm end date (three years) would be sufficient. This too was a compromise, with members like Brajeshwar Prasad eager to keep Parliament out of the picture entirely – 'a House elected on the basis of adult suffrage will consist mostly of persons who are illiterate, and raw. Is it desirable that the question of security of India should be determined by such a House?'[24]

Ambedkar had remained unusually silent during much of the deliberations surrounding emergency provisions. This was uncharacteristic: emergency powers amounted to the Constitution collapsing in on itself, taking along with it Ambedkar's crown jewels, the fundamental rights of citizens. The chapter on fundamental rights was critical to Ambedkar's conceptualization of a democratic state that would do right by its citizens, especially for Scheduled Castes and minorities. Left to itself, even a democratic state might be exclusionary in its ways; only a constitutional mandate to protect the rights of the vulnerable could ensure otherwise. But despite the centrality of fundamental rights in this philosophy, emergency provisions were considered necessary for a more foundational objective – to ensure law and order, without which no individual could exercise their rights in a meaningful manner.

While speaking on the subject of emergency provisions, on the one hand Ambedkar declared that he 'loved fundamental rights', but on the other hand he took refuge in a stray and seldom used provision in the American Constitution that authorized the president to suspend the right to move court through the writ of habeas corpus. Speaking more like a lawyer than a statesman, he dodged the main questions that were asked, bluntly asserted that the safeguards against abuse of emergency power were sufficient, and was perfectly sanguine about empowering the Union at the cost of the State Legislature which could be ordered out of existence.

Excessive questioning by members visibly irritated him. 'Obviously if the Parliament is called and the Proclamation [of Emergency] is placed before it, it would be a stupid thing if the people who come into the Parliament do not take positive action and such a Parliament would be an unnecessary thing and not wanted.'[25] Calling the actions of future parliamentarians 'stupid' was hardly parliamentary and certainly unexpected of Ambedkar. But the debate on emergency provisions had demonstrated a salient truth: when it came to matters relating to powers of federal versus local governments, Ambedkar was an advocate of a big, powerful Centre that would rise above the pettiness of local politics. An empowered and absolutist Centre was desirable at best, a lesser evil than venal local governments at worst.

With Ambedkar's blessing, the chapter on emergency powers, specifically the power to dissolve a State Legislature and rule it directly from New Delhi, sailed through the Assembly. The majority of its members were supportive of its absolute nature, others remained neutral. The minority of dissenting members who were hoping for a meaningful debate were left clutching at straws, their cries in the wilderness now consigned to the ears of future generations. '[Even] when two world wars were fought, the right to approach the High Courts of this country for certain fundamental rights were not taken away . . . ,' said Krishna Chandra Sharma.[26] Its dire impact on the optics of a democratic constitution were made clear: 'if the power is given to the President to abrogate this right [habeas corpus], it will be a slur on the Constitution,' thundered Shibban Lal Saksena; 'the grand affirmation' of fundamental rights was undone by 'the great negation' of emergency powers, said H.V. Kamath.[27]

The ultimate irony, according to H.N. Kunzru, was that Section 93 of the Government of India Act, authorizing the colonial governor to take over the functions of an elected provincial legislature – from which the framers derived the concept of dissolving the State Legislature in an emergency – itself had been deleted by the British before they left India. In the India (Provisional Constitution) Order, 1947, that adapted the Government of India Act for independent India, the governor-general of India had removed this provision, presumably believing such emergency power would be antithetical to the functioning of representative popular democracy.[28] But now, the Constituent Assembly, of its own free will, had resurrected it. The bitter disappointment with Ambedkar and his fellow drafters was mournfully captured by Kamath when the emergency chapter was finally passed: 'This is a day of sorrow and shame. May god help the Indian people.'[29] The colonial constitution had well and truly come alive.

PART II

ALTERNATIVES

FOUR

Bharat

Gandhian ideas about the Constitution centred around fundamental duties over fundamental rights and village unit-led governance over a powerful Union government. But with Gandhi himself preferring consensus over change when it came to the Constitution, these radical ideas were never seriously considered as alternatives to the draft Constitution of India.

The curiosity of free India adopting, enacting, and giving to itself a colonial constitution was compounded by the fact that a home-grown alternative was available. Not only was it simply available but it was also championed by the prospective Father of the Nation, Mahatma Gandhi. Gandhi's vision of a constitution for free India was remarkable in its difference from existing Western notions of what a constitution ought to look like – there was no separation of powers between the legislature, the executive, and the judiciary, no division of power between Centre and states, no fundamental rights as they were commonly understood. These features, if embodied in a new constitution would, according to him, lead to 'English rule without the Englishman', 'the tiger's nature without the tiger', 'not Hindustan but Englistan'.[1]

Instead, in Gandhi's constitutional vision, India was a confederation of self-sufficient villages. Villages would be the basic units of governance enforcing duties on every resident to engage in constructive work. This would ordinarily include whatever people were good at: khadi production, cattle breeding, agriculture, indigenous industry, and so on. In addition, Congress workers in the village would be duty-bound to enforce total prohibition, serve Harijans, boycott foreign cloth, and ensure that all core national activities as determined by the Congress from time to time were carried out in the village.

If a constitution was one of the markers of a civilized society, Gandhi believed that India had nothing to learn from anybody else. India's constitution that had been built over millennia placed men of God above men of war, privileged ethics over power, duties above rights, inherent virtue over artificial restraints of the law. 'A nation with a Constitution like this is fitter to teach others than to learn from others,' Gandhi wrote.[2]

To a constitutional draftsman, these might seem like the values on which a new Constitution of India was to be founded. If ethics were to be privileged over power, a constitutional draftsman would translate that understanding by creating the post of chief ethics officer to advise the prime minister and the cabinet on the exercise of all powers. Such posts could be created in every department of government to ensure that all power was exercised ethically. A conglomeration of chief ethics officers would collectively form the chief ethics council that would be responsible for codifying and regularly updating a code of ethics for the exercise of sovereign power.

But for Gandhi, the values themselves were more important than their translation into a legal text. He was the moral compass, guiding the nation in a journey to discover the values that would nourish it and give it strength. The constitution would take effect later once the nation became 'conscious of its own strength'.[3]

The clearest expression of his priority was in his work *The Constructive Programme*, a book written in 1941.[4] Unlike *Hind Swaraj*, written three decades earlier, *The Constructive Programme* was a categorical affirmation of the significance of morality in building an Independent India. Coming at a time when independence seemed possible, if not imminent, the turn away from the political to the moral took many by surprise. For Gandhi, however, this was neither a digression nor a sudden revelation. On the contrary, it was the culmination of his thoughts on the foundations for independent India.

The Constructive Programme was a social manifesto of sorts with duties assigned to every individual which, if executed, would lead to India attaining 'complete independence by truthful and non-violent means'.[5] The duties encompassed one hour of voluntary daily labour, men treating women as equal comrades in service, the rich taking care of the poor, adhering to the doctrine of trusteeship, and suchlike. There were also rules of economic organization – self-sustaining villages with khadi as the primary industry supported by other cottage industries like soap and match making, a supplement to nationalized industries with constructive and non-violent labour unions – of cultivation of civic virtue by keeping one's villages clean, and of orienting education towards creating model villagers and citizens.

These directions to citizens were founded on two definitive rules of political organization: first, the necessity of devolving power to villages; second, focusing on individual duties rather than rights. For Gandhi, legislative assemblies were 'artificial entities' out of tune with the ethos of the country. With such assemblies, achieving complete independence or functioning as an independent country would be impossible. In contrast, politically and economically autonomous village units could function as basic units of governance. Each village would be administered by a village panchayat: a group of five villagers (male or female) who would be directly elected by all adult residents of the village on an annual basis. This body would exercise legislative, executive, and judicial functions; for instance, it would determine the measure and mode of taxes to be paid by villagers, collect these taxes, and mete out punishment for failure to pay. Using these taxes, the panchayat would draw up and implement development plans, schemes, and laws in sectors such as nutrition, agriculture, public health, sanitation, education, etc. where, according to Gandhi, only residents of a village were in a position to appreciate their unique needs.[6] All villagers would have to serve compulsorily as village guards on a rotational basis, maintaining order through non-violence and satyagraha.[7] In addition to being politically autonomous, each village would be economically independent. All the daily needs of a village were to be met, as far as possible, from its own produce. Where necessary, villages could establish trade relations with each other; for example, Gandhi felt that villages in the Deccan could rely on villages in the Konkan region for salt and coconuts.[8]

The members of the village panchayat would elect the members of the taluka panchayat, which, in turn, would elect the district panchayat, ultimately culminating in a national body – where each body derived its legitimacy from that which elected it. Real political and economic power would be vested in the humble village, a far cry from Delhi. But while self-sufficiency certainly has its appeal, the existence of thousands of politically and economically autonomous units requires elaborate mechanisms for coordination and tools for conflict resolution. What if villages that produce essential commodities refuse to trade with each other? What if villages make rules that are conflicting – say, caste-based occupations are outlawed in one village that takes its Gandhian philosophy seriously, but permitted in another? How would these be resolved? Gandhi himself was the first to admit that he had not dwelled on these difficulties,[9] choosing instead to present an outline of village-centric governance. The village was the antithesis of Delhi, which for Gandhi was 'perched on Mt. Everest' in relation to the rest of India.[10] It was uniquely unsuited to make laws for the whole country.

Village governments, being closest to the people, were also the most legitimate institutions for implementing one of the fundamental planks of Gandhian thought: the duties of individuals towards the state and to each other. For Gandhi, the Bhagavad Gita was a masterful treatise on doing one's duty, irrespective of its consequences. It was this metaphysical understanding of duty that Gandhi sought to make real in his political struggle.

In the political sphere in colonial India, the duty of a citizen primarily operated as a duty to pay taxes to the British government. As a result, the demand of citizens centred not around the notion of duty, but instead on the notion of rights. This was a tradition dating back to the French Revolution: oppressed citizens demanding their rights as men and women equal before the law. It built on an even older canon of liberal thought that spoke of the rights of man by virtue of his very existence. In

India too, the articulation of demands for self-rule and independence took the form of a demand for rights. The Karachi Resolution of 1931 summed up this demand in the form of seven fundamental rights to speech, association, religion, bearing arms, equality, and non-discrimination both in public places and public employment.[11]

Gandhi endorsed the Karachi Resolution unequivocally. Yet, unlike the traditional Western canon, which sees rights and duties as 'jural opposites'[12]– one person's right means another person's duty – for Gandhi, 'the true source of rights is duty'.[13] Channelling Krishna in the Mahabharata, Gandhi believed that everyone's duty is to act; rights are merely the fruits of that action. For the conceptual purist, this philosophical relation might have raised several eyebrows. Would the right to speak freely in democratic India depend on whether one had paid taxes? Could only those who had sung the national anthem in the morning have the right to travel across the country? Gandhi may not have intellectually extended his thought all the way through. For him, it was a useful juxtaposition that allowed him to advocate for rights politically while stressing on duties of individuals as the foundation of an independent, non-violent nation state.

Borrowing from Keats, performing a duty for Gandhi was 'a thing of beauty and a joy for ever'.[14] However in the same breath he added 'the awful fact, however, has often been to know where duty lies'.[15] This required deep introspection and understanding of oneself. Gandhi didn't consider it his brief to provide a checkbox of duties for every individual. Instead, he simply stated that the most fundamental duty was to follow the path of truth and non-violence. Since this requires immense self-discipline, particularly when dealing with members of the community and the state, the constitution of the polity into village units would bring the state closest to the people. This, in turn, would make the citizen–state relationship a personal one based on mutually reinforcing duties. Citizens would owe a duty to be truthful, the state in turn would act faithfully in the interest of its citizens.

This vision of the state as a beneficent guardian taking care of its citizen wards was such a far cry from anything that had ever existed as a matter of verifiable historical fact that it seemed whimsical to even suggest it as a practical matter. Citizens weren't always dutiful children and rulers were rarely only motivated by the welfare of their citizens. Taking the state closer through village governments may have bridged this distance somewhat. But it is not as if villages were homogeneous units where amity and harmony perpetually prevailed. There were differences in caste, class, occupation, gendered roles for men and women outside and inside the home, all of which made villages layered and complex settings. Gandhi was theoretically right: being small and self-contained, villages may have provided the best shot for harmonious coexistence. But he ignored a salient truth emerging out of the history of political violence in India – the intimate neighbour could easily morph into a political enemy.[16]

To brush the complexity and history of India's village life aside would be to base a new constitution on make-believe. That is why in drafting an actual constitution, a focus on a metaphysical understanding of duty in an idealized village unit would not take one very far. Gandhi thought so too – a constitution was a policy document, 'essentially a temporary expedient which one might alter as circumstances altered'.[17] A son could never fulfil his filial duties as a matter of policy, Gandhi said. It would only happen if he was truthful to his parents. Simply because India became independent, no policy could transform it overnight, no matter how noble its goals. Giving the example of the Karachi Resolution, he said that despite the resolution stating that there shall be no untouchability, the practice had continued; barring liquor and drugs shops did not mean drugs and drink vanished, the categorical affirmation of equality did not lead to Hindus, Muslims, and Christians giving up their distrust and suspicion of each other.[18] Simply stating these principles would not automatically lead to justice. It would require individuals to be truthful to their creed and convert these words into a living reality. That was not in the realm of the Constitution but in the realm of a man's creed. That is where Gandhi's primary interest lay.

Gandhian Constitutions

For Gandhi, certain constitutions captured his creed better than others. One such constitution was that of Aundh, a tiny princely state on the outskirts of modern-day Pune, with a population of approximately 75,000 at the time.[19] Bhawanrao Pant Pratinidhi, the maharaja of Aundh, had established a responsible government, becoming in the process a titular king.[20] The democratization of Aundh had begun as early as 1923, with the establishment of a legislative council to advise the maharaja. In 1938 a charter was proclaimed deepening democratic relations between the ruler and his subjects. The charter was authored by Maurice Frydman,[21] an engineer turned hermit who took part in Aundh's democratic experiment as an adviser. A year later, Aundh's constitution – a remarkably original document said to have been based on principles dictated personally by Gandhi to the maharaja[22] – came into force.

Heavily influenced by Gandhian thought, self-sufficient village communities were the anchor of a decentralized state machinery in Aundh's constitution. Each village was administered by a directly elected gram panchayat headed by a sarpanch, chosen collectively by the panchayat.[23] The formal legal system with lawyers and courts was abolished and justice delivery was made the responsibility of the Nyaaya Sabha, a local body.[24] For complex matters including criminal cases, there was only one high court judge to hear and adjudicate disputes.[25] The constitution gave every citizen of Aundh a wide array of fundamental rights – life, equality, basic education, employment, minimum wages, freedom of expression, peaceful assembly, and worship – subject to public morality and non-violence.[26] While it required citizens to be literate to be able to vote, the constitution also obligated the state to provide free primary education to all citizens, ensuring that no one was disenfranchised.[27] The constitution operated in Aundh for nearly a decade till the princely state's merger with independent India on 8 March 1948.

Hailing the Aundh Constitution, Gandhi called it a 'noble example'[28] which he hoped would be copied by other states. But he was equally aware of Aundh's size and the difficulty of replication in larger states with established administrative machineries, let alone the whole of India. This is why despite praising Aundh's efforts, Gandhi didn't take it further or make a serious attempt to incorporate its learnings for a national constitution.

Instead, the most notable attempt in this regard was made by the devout Gandhian Shriman Narayan

Agarwal.[29] Championing a radical bottom-up constitution, Agarwal's work was based on the founding tenets of Gandhian thought – decentralized government and rights contingent on duties. These were based on a philosophical view that the Western binary between individuals and the state was misleading: individuals were as much part of the state and ought to perform duties to the state as duties to oneself. Similar obligations towards individuals would be borne by the state. Recognizing that a large state inevitably leads to a disjunct and a reappearance of the citizen–state binary, he instead advocated for 'well-knit and coordinated village communities with their positive and direct democracy, non-violent cottage economy and human contacts'.[30]

Going back to village republics was not a call to become primitive again. Neither was it inward-looking. Self-contained village communities would not be islands unto themselves but rather parts of a larger whole. For an example of this, Agarwal held up the janapadas of the Chola empire, large gatherings of community councils to take significant decisions of the state. Villages in the Chola empire were integrated into the larger whole in a pyramidal structure starting from the base with direct representation in the form of the janapadas. Inspired by this, Agarwal's constitution espoused village panchayats, the president of which would be part of an advisory taluka panchayat to be replicated successively to comprise Parliament. As a result, every member of Parliament would also be a member of every governing body right down to the village panchayat. This would ensure that they remained directly accountable to the people, unlike a centralized government where parliamentarians sat atop Everest in Delhi while their constituents scurried about in the rest of the nation below.

In this inverted structure, supreme state power to make laws and execute them was wielded by the village panchayat, each successive unit responsible only for coordination and advice. In the village panchayat, governance was akin to that of a direct democracy, the panchayat responding directly to the sentiments of the people of the village. The upshot of such village-level autonomy was that every village could potentially formulate rules on a range of matters to suit their own interests. In one village, the age of marriage may be set at twelve, in another at eighteen; in one village, cow slaughter may be banned, in another the skin of old, unproductive cows may be considered a source of significant income – the possibilities of differences in rules were potentially limitless. Clearly, in such cases, the coordination function to be performed by the units above the village panchayat would be critical. After all, it would hardly be a desirable state of affairs if young men and women from one village had to elope to another one to get married. Gandhi had frankly stated that he had not thought about these practical difficulties, leaving them to be worked out in the future. But when that time came, Agarwal's draft remained silent on how such coordination would happen and conflicts resolved. Instead, like Gandhi himself, the justification offered was a principled one – a return to such village-based administration would be a return to a form of government 'instinctive to India'.[31]

Such a hyperlocal form of government would also be necessary to sustain Agarwal's Gandhian formulation that all fundamental rights in the Constitution would be contingent on the performance of certain duties. These included contributing funds or labour to the state, resisting exploiting other individuals, and a general duty of remaining faithful to the state.[32] From a simple reading of these duties, it is evident that these are moral guides rather than legal claims. It was a reimagination of the very idea of what a constitution is and how it is to be enforced. One might have countenanced such a possibility as a thought experiment, but Agarwal made fundamental rights, including those considered widely salient to human existence such as equality, non-discrimination, and free speech, contingent on the performance of duties. Did that mean that a citizen could not claim equality unless she had contributed monetarily to the state? Was conscription a precondition to free speech? These were frightening possibilities. Equally frightening would be the prospect of how the state would enforce such duties. How would the state know whether an individual had been faithful or not? Would it involve citizens being under constant surveillance or would there be periodic tests to ascertain faithfulness? Agarwal, perhaps wisely, remained silent on these critical details too.

Taken to its logical conclusion, the Gandhian constitution quickly unravels into a potential charter of oppression. This was less the fault of Shriman Agarwal and more a product of conflating moral guidance with a legal document. Unsurprisingly, Gandhi himself realized this acutely. In writing the foreword to a constitution that bore his name, Gandhi was quick to deny subtly but surely the slightest hint of authorship. While praising the author for his efforts, he pointedly remarked that the title may be misleading as it is neither a document that he could 'commit to' nor was this really a constitution. Instead, it contained some broad guidelines on what a constitution that incorporates Gandhian thought might look like. But, as he reiterated, a reader should not make the mistake of taking the title literally, as a constitution whose every detail had Gandhi's unqualified endorsement.[33]

It, however, wasn't the case that Shriman Agarwal used a provocative title simply to sell a few extra copies. Gandhi was in reasonably regular touch with Agarwal, had read his manuscript on more than one occasion, and had made several suggestions. In an early letter he had also chided him saying the manuscript required 'more hard work and careful thinking'.[34] Yet when the book was actually published, despite having spent considerable time and energy in shaping its contents, Gandhi equivocated while writing the foreword. Agarwal's work and its obvious conceptual limitations may have justified such equivocation. However, equivocation in relation to constitutional questions wasn't new for Gandhi; in fact, it was more Gandhian than Agarwal's earnest attempt to incorporate his ideas in a constitutional framework.

Gandhian Pragmatism

Gandhi's equivocation regarding the substance of constitutions was discernible from his reaction to the constitutional recommendations made by the Motilal Nehru Committee in 1928. The Nehru Report is widely viewed as the first constitutional document for India by Indians. It was devised by an All Parties Conference of diverse representatives including Subhas Chandra Bose, Ali Imam, Tej Bahadur Sapru, Shuaib Qureshi, and M.S. Aney with Motilal Nehru as chairman and Jawaharlal as secretary.

In both its diverse representation and its contents, it

was a precursor to the Constitution of India – featuring fundamental rights, a parliamentary form of government, division of powers between the Centre and provinces, a unified judiciary with a new Supreme Court above the high courts, and the concept of reservations for uplift of certain groups. In short, it was a clear repudiation of Gandhian concepts of village units and fundamental duties as the building blocks for democracy.

Yet when writing about the report in *Young India*, Gandhi spoke less about its contents and more about the fact that it had been unanimously adopted by the All Parties Conference: '[T]he main thing was not to present perfect recommendations but to secure unanimity for the recommendations that might in the circumstances be considered the best possible.' He encouraged those who would consider the report for adoption to desist from a critical examination but rather 'to see the thing through'.[35]

This was not because Gandhi did not believe a critical examination of the report to be worth his while. In a letter to Zafar-ul-Mulk, he clarified that he had indeed examined it and found the Constitution 'entirely Western'.[36] But he was quick to justify its Westernness by saying that the Constitution can only be a 'logical outcome of the institutions we have at present'. For Gandhi, this was not a reason to decry the document. If it was found unsuitable by Indians over time, he was certain that another constitution would be drafted in its place. For the present, it was a 'passable Constitution' which had produced a 'tolerable agreement' amongst all parties. This was reason enough for him to recommend it wholeheartedly for adoption.

When it came to the Constitution, Gandhi's reactions were usually characterized by such pragmatism, forsaking exalted principles. This is why Gandhi had himself moved the resolution on fundamental rights in the Karachi session of the Congress in 1931.[37] For Gandhi, this resolution was only meant to delineate the contours of Ram Rajya (the ideal state) without getting into 'intricate questions of the Constitution'. This was a surprise since in the Gandhian framework, Ram Rajya would be achieved with an emphasis on duties and not rights. Yet he actively moved a resolution that dealt with a range of civil and political rights – free speech, free association, freedom of religion, socio-economic rights, no serfdom, a living wage, protection of women workers, etc. None of these rights would be conditional on the performance of any duties as Gandhi had himself advocated in *Hind Swaraj*, a credo dutifully adhered to in the Gandhian constitution by Agarwal. When it came to the drafting of the real thing, Gandhi chose consensus over conviction.

This was why in the Ramgarh session of the Congress

in 1940, Gandhi led the call for the establishment of a Constituent Assembly to draft a constitution for India.[38] This was a radical volte-face – Gandhi had greeted earlier resolutions moved by Jawaharlal Nehru on this matter with considerable scepticism. Writing in the *Harijan* in 1939, however, Gandhi explained the change he had undergone: he no longer saw the Constitution primarily as a legal text laying down binding rights and duties but rather as a 'remedy for our communal and other distempers' as well as a 'vehicle for mass political and other education'.[39] It mattered less that the Constitution which would emerge from such an Assembly would not be ideal or perfect; what was significant was that, in his words, it would 'be real'.[40] More importantly, all communities would be represented in its making in the exact proportion of their populations as all major parties had agreed.

In terms of its content, it would provide for universal adult franchise, giving every person, irrespective of their literacy levels, property ownership, sex, or religion, one vote. In 1940, with the Muslim League having built up its support amongst Muslims on the ground and clashing regularly with the Congress on policy matters, Gandhi saw the potential of a Constituent Assembly with representation of all communities as the great unifier. Moreover, as he said evocatively, it was 'the only way out'.[41]

When finally in 1946 the Constituent Assembly was

convened, its first significant act was to pass the Objectives Resolution – a preamble of sorts, unequivocally declaring India's imminent sovereignty and right to determine its own future, as well as setting out the Assembly's vision for the country and its constitution. It asserted that the people were sovereign, declared that the government would be federal with states holding a large share of power, and promised justice, equality, and freedoms for all. It set India and its Constituent Assembly on the path of creating a constitution along the lines of its predecessors elsewhere: focusing on guarantees of rights and equality, separation of powers between the Centre and the states, wrapped in the uplifting rhetoric of freedom, independence, and a prominent place for India in the new world order. Conspicuously absent from its contents was any mention of fundamental duties of citizens or empowered village panchayats, pillars of the Gandhian constitution.

This omission was neither oversight nor unbeknownst to Gandhi. In fact, the Objectives Resolution emerged from an Experts Committee set up by the Congress Working Committee in anticipation of the Constituent Assembly. In its recommendations, the Experts Committee came up with a draft objectives resolution (called a 'declaration') which in nearly verbatim form became the ultimate Objectives Resolution passed by the Constituent Assembly. This resolution was expressly approved by the Congress party on the eve of the summoning of the Constituent Assembly. Speaking a month later in Srirampur, Gandhi endorsed the resolution, saying that it had been moved keeping in mind the need for 'justice to all communities'.[42] Gandhi the constitutional realist was at work again.

The Objectives Resolution would set the course for the work of the Constituent Assembly and the future shape of the Constitution itself. If the nation had to be fundamentally recast into a bottom-up republic with an emphasis on fundamental duties of all citizens, the resolution would have to contain the kernel of that transformation. Practical politics, however, meant that the winter of 1946 was not the time for idealized notions of what a constitution ought to be for Gandhi. The Muslim League had refused to join the Constituent Assembly, and without them, its entire legitimacy was at stake. It was critical for Gandhi and the Congress to try to entice them or manoeuvre them back into the fold. The Objectives Resolution held out an olive branch, promising a federal India with provinces having autonomous powers as the Cabinet Mission had recommended. The rest of the document contained homilies to rights, justice, and sovereignty that no right-thinking person could have any serious objection to. That may not have been the case if a radically altered bottom-up, fundamentally duty-centric

Gandhian constitution had been prepared. Gandhi and the Congress played safe with the Objectives Resolution. This decision meant that any chance of a Gandhian constitution was foreclosed.

This is why ardent followers of Gandhian principles who were members of the Constituent Assembly were caught in a bind: the proposed Constitution itself was a far cry from what the Mahatma had envisioned, yet Gandhi himself had supported the framework of the Constitution under discussion and urged the adoption of the Objectives Resolution. Unsurprisingly, the debate on the Objectives Resolution in the Constituent Assembly largely steered clear of references to Gandhi. Once the Mahatma had endorsed it, for Gandhians in the Assembly to point out how un-Gandhian it was could only cause him embarrassment. Critical engagement was substituted by hoary platitudes to the momentous nature of the resolution, rather than its contents.

Once the conceptual trajectory of the drafting process was set with the passage of the Objectives Resolution, it was only a matter of time before the practical realism of a constitution along those lines prevailed over the radical and only partially articulated idealism of a Gandhian one. As per Gandhi's instructions, avowed Congressmen in the Assembly, particularly those who swore by Gandhian ideals, participated fully in deliberations. On certain matters they were able to influence the content of the Constitution. Untouchability abolition, a prohibition on alcohol, a ban on cow slaughter were all parts of the Gandhian playbook that made their way to the final document. But the key principles of a Gandhian constitution – decentralized government based on village panchayats and an equal emphasis on fundamental duties as fundamental rights – remained absent.

For committed Gandhians in the Assembly, this was a hard pill to swallow. As the intricacies of the Constitution were worked out in committee rooms, Gandhian Assembly members, while being faithful participants, had overriding priorities elsewhere. For Patel, there was a country to govern, for B.G. Kher, Bombay state had to be administered, Pattabhi Sitaramayya took over the reins of the Congress party and remained by Gandhi's side. The actual drafting of the Constitution was left to the committees, to be shepherded by Ambedkar, chairman of the Drafting Committee.

When this committee put together a draft Constitution for deliberation in the Assembly, those with Gandhian leanings reacted in two distinct ways. Some, like Kher and Sitaramayya, claimed the Constitution was in fact Gandhian, choosing to focus on matters like prohibition which found a place in the chapter on directive principles. Others like them, including Durgabai Deshmukh and Satish Chandra, said that if one approached the Constitution with a Gandhian spirit of service, one could make of it what one wished. It wouldn't be an overstatement to say that they were clutching at straws.

More thoughtful commentators, however, had a deep sense of distress that the Constitution in its final form was not Gandhian at all. Kengal Hanumanthaiah, member of the Assembly and future chief minister of Mysore state, minced no words when he famously said that the Constitution resembled neither the music of the veena nor the sitar, but an English band. In true Gandhian fashion, he followed this up by saying that it wasn't the fault of those who drafted the Constitution but those like him in the Assembly 'who entrusted them with this kind of work'.[43] Specifically disappointing for Hanumanthaiah was the top-down nature of the Constitution. 'The pyramid has been reversed,' he said evocatively. Instead of vesting significant power in local bodies, it concentrated power in the Centre with some powers with states. Hanumanthaiah sardonically observed that for the framers, the path to democracy in India ran only through Delhi, much like the Hindu dogma that the only path to heaven is through 'a dip in the river Ganges, especially at Benares' and nowhere else![44]

Equally disappointed was Shankarrao Deo, long-time Gandhian and general secretary of the Congress party. Deo had been a key participant in the Aundh experiment where a bottom-up Gandhian democracy had been established.[45] Not only did that experiment fail to shape the framing of the Constitution of India, but also its spirit of an authentic, decentralized governance model was lost on the framers. This, Deo believed, happened because the framers of the Constitution of India were 'constitutional pandits', none of whom had been part of the revolutionary struggle that preceded Independence. 'The Constitution can hardly be called the "child" of the Indian revolution,' Deo said wistfully. While it had 'every institution which guarantees liberty to man, every principle which promotes progress and fraternity', yet it did not contain any 'machinery for the implementation of any definite principle of progress inspiring our Revolution'.[46]

This, Deo was quick to add, was not a reflection on the Constitution framers but rather the people themselves who had failed to fully internalize the Gandhian ideal of a non-violent society based on local governance and self-sufficient villages. Unsurprisingly, the Constitution reflected the status quo. As a result, it emerged as a patchwork of provisions from different countries in the world. It promised a 'third alternative' to the world – a non-violent and equal society – but ended up being carried away by established doctrines of cabinet government from Britain, checks and balances from the

United States, and the winds of centralization of power that were blowing worldwide at the time. As a result, it had little original to offer the world in return. Deo spoke for a large section of the Constituent Assembly when he said, '[I]t is the fault of us all, because we have not faithfully followed our Master.'[47]

As Gandhi had himself said on multiple occasions, the Constitution that would be adopted by India would ultimately be the product of its circumstances. On 26 November 1949, when the Constituent Assembly finally enacted the Constitution of independent India, the country had just undergone a bloody partition, was struggling to lift its citizenry out of abject poverty, but was filled with hope that with autonomy and self-rule, a new dawn would emerge. The Constitution laid the foundation for that dawn in a way the framers thought best: by taking the best the world had to offer and allowing it to be shaped for Indian circumstances by vesting power in responsible Indian officials. This was the prevalent belief in Indian intelligentsia, consequently becoming the default consensus shared across the political spectrum. Such consensus mattered to Gandhi much more at that critical time than the contents of an ideal Gandhian constitution. That would have to wait its turn.

In retrospect, the Constitution of India that came into force in 1950 was neither a decisive break from the past nor transformative. The former might have been the case if Gandhi's ideas had carried the day. But that was not to be. Despite being enacted in the shadow of the greatest non-violent freedom struggle in history, its drafting appeared to have proceeded on a parallel track to the struggle, imbued with neither its radicalism nor its novelty. It had its share of bold thoughts – on reservations, economic democracy, and freedom of religion in particular – but on the whole it eschewed originality for stability, novelty for wisdom, and the spirit of revolution for the spirit of continuity. It was a colonial constitution that was expected to lead to a new dawn for postcolonial India.

FIVE

Hindusthan

The Constitution of the Hindusthan Free State endorsed by the All India Hindu Mahasabha was very similar in concept to the Constitution of India. There was no Hindutva-based alternative to the colonial constitution.

What might a Hindutva constitution look like? In the mid-1940s, this was a question that neither the Hindu Mahasabha nor the RSS had ever seriously considered. Though both were Hindutvavadi groups, in relative terms, they were new entities. The Mahasabha began as a grouping within the Congress, only carving out an independent identity in 1928. The RSS, set up in 1925, was explicitly concerned with the socio-cultural revival of Hindus, particularly their ability to defend themselves. A constitution was remote to the organizational priorities of both these institutions.

With the victory of the Liberal Party in Britain in 1906, the colonial government was considering a slew of political reforms that would enable Indians to elect their own representatives to provincial legislative councils. But the failure of Hindus to organize themselves had meant that there was no effective voice to represent Hindu interests within the Congress, or to the British directly. The Hindu Mahasabha emerged out of the Punjab Hindu Sabha set up in 1907 by prominent Punjabi Hindus. Explaining the reason for its establishment, Lala Lajpat Rai, one of its prime architects, said plainly that there were many issues, such as the use of the Sanskrit language, preventing proselytization of Hindu orphans, and cow protection, which mattered to all Hindus. For Rai and leaders of the Punjab Hindu Sabha, Hindus were a distinct people with their own culture and community practices distinct from Muslims. The Muslims too had recognized this and set up the Muslim League earlier in the decade to advocate their interests. Rai found this 'perfectly justified' as they were only 'looking to the interests of their own community'.[1] Hindus now needed an outfit of their own.

Soon it was clear that these issues that mattered to Hindus were not limited to Punjab. In the United Provinces, Bengal, and other areas where Arya Samajists and Sanatan Dharm organizations had a wide following, the mission of the Punjab Hindu Sabha found resonance. Pandit Madan Mohan Malaviya took the lead, and after a few stillborn attempts, in 1915, the All India Hindu Sabha was convened on the sidelines of the Kumbh Mela in Haridwar. It renamed itself the All India Hindu Mahasabha in 1921, to underline that it was a representative body encompassing all Hindu sabhas that had previously been established.

For Rai, Madan Mohan Malaviya, and other early leaders of the Hindu Mahasabha, organizing Hindus was an activity within the larger umbrella of the Congress party. From 1922, the Sabha itself functioned on the sidelines of the Congress sessions. All members of the Sabha were usually also members of the Congress. For its members, there was no dissonance between functioning as members of both entities. The Hindu Mahasabha was set up to unite Hindus within the Congress and shape Congress policies. It was not a dissident faction.

Over time, however, notable fissures started to appear. With the ascendancy of Gandhi in the Congress, members of the Mahasabha expressed their disapproval of the practice of non-cooperation. Non-cooperation involved the deliberate disregard of British laws, a strategy that members of the Mahasabha were opposed to. Over time, Gandhi's concession of reserved seats in legislatures for Dalit groups and the extension of an olive branch to the Muslim League with a view to forging national unity did not sit well with Mahasabha leaders.[2] In 1928, for the first time, the Mahasabha session was held in Jabalpur and not on the sidelines of the Congress session in Calcutta. The decisive break was caused by the Congress decision to endorse the British proposal to separate Sind from the province of Bombay. The Mahasabha members opposed this in categorical terms, fearing for the status of Hindu minorities in Muslim-majority Sind as opposed to Hindu-majority Bombay where they now resided.

Matters came to a head with the Communal Award announced by British prime minister Ramsay MacDonald in 1932. The Award recognized not only Muslims, Christians, and Sikhs, but also the Depressed Classes of Hindus as minorities who would vote for their own representatives through separate electorates. Prior to the Award, this concept of separate electorates had been formally introduced in India through the Indian Councils Act, 1909, by setting up separate electorates only for Muslims.[3] In 1919, after the passage of the first Government of India Act, separate electorates were continued for Muslims and this benefit was also extended to Sikhs, Indian Christians, Anglo-Indians, and Europeans.[4] Gandhi opposed the 1932 Award since he opposed the creation of separate electorates for Depressed Classes, but the Congress remained neutral to it on the whole. It instead sought to find a consensus amongst all parties. The neutrality of the Congress decisively pushed the Mahasabha into building its own organization.

The Emergence of Savarkar

While the Mahasabha was charting its own path away from the Congress, Vinayak Damodar Savarkar was slowly gaining a reputation as an organizer of Hindus in Bombay state. Savarkar had earned his revolutionary stripes as a firebrand nationalist in London. He had been sentenced to transportation for life twice over, amounting to imprisonment for fifty years, at the Cellular Jail in the Andaman and Nicobar Islands. The charges against him were serious – abetment to the murder of the collector of Nashik and waging war against the king.[5] Subsequent to his early release from prison in the Andamans, he repositioned himself as the intellectual fountainhead of Hindu revivalism in national politics.

Hindutva, or Hindu-ness, was for Savarkar the basis for the Indian nation state. His explanation of Hindutva was complex, perhaps a key stumbling block for its limited resonance at the time. Hindutva was not a theory of Hinduism; in fact, it had little to do with religious practice at all. It was a political theory that was presented as the foundation of India as a Hindu Rashtra (nation) for the Hindu *jati* (race) representing Hindu *sanskriti* (civilization). Anyone who considered the land between the river Sindhu (Indus) in the north and the Sindhu Sagar (Indian Ocean) in the south as their *pitribhumi* (literally, fatherland; in this case, the land of one's ancestors) and *punyabhumi* (holy land) was a person who, according to Savarkar, was tied by the bond of Hindutva, and hence a Hindu. Only a Hindu as per his definition could, strictly speaking, be an Indian national. This meant that by definition Buddhists, Jains, and Sikhs could be included in a future Hindu state as citizens, but Christians, Muslims, and others who had their holy lands outside India, or those like Parsis, whose ancestors had come from elsewhere, could not. Atheists with ancestors from the Indian subcontinent, however, could also claim to be Hindus since they shared 'a common blood', and by virtue of not having any holy land at all, were part of a 'born brotherhood'.[6]

A largely polemical book, *Essentials of Hindutva*, in which Savarkar formulated the doctrine, was concerned as much with the future Indian nation state as with its past. It was written with the objective of correcting history: how Hindus were actually wronged and did not suffer defeat at the hands of Muslim 'invaders' as is assumed, how their victories were suppressed and defeats highlighted, how Shivaji, Maharana Pratap, and Shalivahana were reduced to footnotes in the annals of history owing to biased historical accounts. Much of this Hindu revivalism was designed to instil pride but also to make Hindus more warrior-like. In fact, in Savarkar's view, the reason Hindus became pacifist and lost their warrior-like nature in the first place was because of the rise of Buddhism with its teachings of peace and universal fraternity. Buddhism, for Savarkar, remained the original sin of Hindu political thought, rendering Hindus weak and unable to defend themselves from alien invasions.

Essentials of Hindutva was written like a historical account, meant to invoke a sense of pride amongst Hindus. Its messaging was complex – Hindu pride was divorced from Hindu religion – but its prime impetus was an instinctive feeling of resentment against Muslims who, as outsiders, had 'invaded' India. There was very little in terms of a positive programme for freeing the Hindu nation from the colonial yoke. When contrasted with Gandhi's mass politics of non-violence coupled with an overt celebration of Hindu rituals, the singing of Vaishnava bhajans, and the promise of Ram Rajya – Savarkar's more esoteric attempt at restoring Hindu pride – remained at the fringes of the national movement.

What the book, however, did was to make Savarkar a leading light in non-Congress politics. His growing stature and tirades against the politics of the Congress led him to the presidency of the Hindu Mahasabha in 1937, a post he held unchallenged and uninterrupted till 1944.[7] During this time, the Mahasabha became part of the provincial government in Bengal in alliance with the Progressive Coalition Party, the Krishak Praja Party, Forward Bloc, and the Independent Scheduled Caste Party.[8] Though this was only possible because of the resignation of the incumbent Congress ministers, it was nonetheless the first time that the Hindu Mahasabha emerged out of the shadows into the political mainstream. Savarkar had given them a clear ideology, and its leading light in Bengal, Shyama Prasad Mookerjee, had taken them into government. It appeared that their time – as an entity to be reckoned with in India's fast-shifting political firmament – had come.

To reinforce its seriousness as a political outfit rivalling the Congress, in the 1939 session of the Hindu Mahasabha in Calcutta, Savarkar laid out his vision of a future constitution of India. In such a constitution, all citizens would have equal rights on the condition that they 'avow and owe an exclusive and devoted allegiance to the Hindusthani state'.[9] This was a deviation from the theory of Hindutva, where even despite such allegiance being declared, a Muslim or Christian could not claim equal citizenship since their holy land factually remained elsewhere. This deviation was not unintentional – the entire edifice of Savarkar's constitutional vision was political acceptability of the Hindu Mahasabha as a mainstream political party. The radical nature of Hindutva ideology would now have to be toned down in an attempt to take on the Congress as the leading force in nationalist politics. Savarkar went further: so that non-Hindus would not feel apprehensive about the Mahasabha, he also stressed that their rights regarding their religion, culture, and language would be expressly guaranteed in the constitution. Minorities could also set up special schools for their children with government support, provided the majority could do the same with proportionate state support. Essentially for Savarkar, communities could maintain their own identities, but everyone was a citizen of Hindusthan first.

Drafting such a constitution was a route for the Hindu Mahasabha to become both politically acceptable and rival the Congress. After the end of the Second World War, the establishment of the Constituent Assembly was imminent. To prepare for this momentous development, it was no longer just desirable but also necessary for all political parties to set out their own vision of the constitution on the basis of which India would be a sovereign nation. Following Savarkar's lead, this is what the Mahasabha set out to do.

Constitution of the Hindusthan Free State

The Mahasabha entrusted the hard task of drafting the actual provisions of a constitutional document to the Bhopatkar Satkar Nidhi in Poona, which functioned as a de facto drafting committee. This group, which was an institution set up by Laxman Bhopatkar,[10] a follower of Bal Gangadhar Tilak and a prominent leader of the Hindu

Mahasabha, set up a committee led by D.V. Gokhale.[11] Intellectual heft was provided by N.C. Kelkar, a well-known nationalist leader from Maharashtra, who had urged Savarkar to take up the presidency of the Mahasabha in the first place.

The constitution that came out of their deliberations optically looked very distinct from the eventual Constitution of India. It was relatively shorter, with 111 provisions. It also contained a set of principles that provided the underlying basis for these provisions. Semantically, it struck a different chord, referring to India as 'Hindusthan' and the constitution as the Constitution of the 'Hindusthan Free State'. The name was a reflection of the study on global constitutions that had been undertaken by the committee. During this study, it emerged that the Irish Free State should be a model, having managed to free itself from British rule two decades earlier. For the draftsmen, borrowing the title 'free state' would mark a decisive break from any kind of subservience, whether to colonial rule or even to the Commonwealth, much like the Irish Free State had managed. The drafters did not make any bones about their borrowed inspiration: after all, in their words, India was 'the last in the British Empire to seek emancipation through a democratic and republican constitution'.[12]

What was also borrowed were the principles on

which the constitution was founded. These principles proclaimed popular sovereignty, individual freedom, justice and peace, and indivisibility of the nation state as the founding tenets of the new nation. The drafters adopted these principles because they were the distillation of 'modern political thought'.[13] Undoubtedly, the first three could claim this mantle and had formed the bedrock of all well-meaning twentieth-century constitutions. The fourth principle of the indivisibility of the Indian nation state was a reflection of the Hindu Mahasabha's steadfast opposition to the idea of Pakistan and the partition of India.[14] Hindusthan was a land which, for Savarkar and the Mahasabha, was geographically bounded by the Himalayas and the great mountains of the north and the Indian Ocean in the south. The fact that some areas had a Muslim majority was irrelevant; their constitution provided adequate safeguards to ensure the protection of all minority communities in the future Hindusthan Free State. Muslims had no reason to worry, let alone press for partition to secure their future.

Given the extent of borrowing, it was unsurprising that the substance of the Constitution of the Hindusthan Free State was as colonially inspired as the eventual Constitution of India. The starting point for Gokhale and his colleagues, much like it was for Rau and Ambedkar, was a study of global constitutions. The Soviet Constitution apart, at the time, there was a global consensus on what civilized democracies should enshrine in constitutional texts. Fundamental rights of citizens were the bedrock of such texts.

While incorporating fundamental rights, the Constitution of the Hindusthan Free State expressly acknowledged the Four Freedoms enumerated by President Roosevelt as its chief inspiration.[15] These were the civil and political freedoms of expression and worship, and the socio-economic freedoms from want and fear. Not restrained by legalistic objections of whether the latter would be feasible for the state to provide, the Constitution of the Hindusthan Free State made the right to receive free education, insurance against unemployment, living wage to every worker, maternity benefits, old age pensions, and land rights to the tiller guaranteed 'rights of man and citizen'.[16]

Unlike those who drafted the Constitution of India, the drafters of the Constitution of the Hindusthan Free State were not unduly concerned by the practical question of how such rights, which required significant state resources, would be realized. They were also not as wary of possible claims in court flowing from non-enforcement. Kelkar, the author of a twenty-nine-page foreword to the fifty-six-page constitution[17] and one of its chief endorsers, had himself trained as a lawyer but had really made his career as the editor of *Kesari* and *Mahratta*, nationalist publications brought out from Poona. He was a long-time associate of Lokmanya Tilak, and after Tilak's death, a reluctant Gandhian.[18] Later, he split with Gandhi over the issue of non-cooperation – like many he felt that responsive cooperation with the British would be a more fruitful method of achieving the demands of the national movement. For him, the constitution was an ideal political charter to lay out the Mahasabha's vision for India; he had no desire to get caught up in the details of how that vision would become reality. As a result, it sometimes appeared like a fanciful wish list.

The most intriguing element where the Constitution of the Hindusthan Free State broadly matched the eventual Constitution of India related to the freedom of religion. With Savarkar's well-established understanding of Hindutva as the basis for a future Indian nation state, there was no real place for Muslims, Christians, Jews, and Parsis to be equal citizens in such a state. It might have been expected that the constitution endorsed by the Mahasabha would incorporate such an idea. This might have taken the form of two classes of citizenship, with preference given to those adhering to the Hindu faith, as defined by Savarkar. But the Constitution of the Hindusthan Free State contained none of these ideas. Instead, it provided freedom of conscience, free profession, and practice of religion for all. Further, it guaranteed to every citizen the protection of their culture and language, subject only to public order and morality. The state was also prohibited from discriminating against anyone on the basis of their religious belief or status. Religious instruction could not be forced on anyone in a school receiving public grants. Finally, it was categorically declared that there would be no state religion in the Hindusthan Free state. This restricted religion to a protected private sphere and foreclosed the possibility of a constitutional Hindu Rashtra.

If Hindutva was to function as a theory of state formation, as Savarkar had intended, it would have to be reflected in provisions on citizenship in a future constitution. But the Constitution of the Hindusthan Free State did not create categories of citizens. On the contrary, it read like a standard liberal constitution, of the kind that ultimately formed the foundation of the Constitution of India. This move by the Mahasabha to the political middle was undoubtedly a sacrifice of ideology at the altar of political acceptability. It also had much to do with the rise of the RSS.

The Rise of the RSS

By the Bilaspur session in 1944, when the Hindu Mahasabha passed a resolution to draft a Constitution of the Hindusthan Free State, its political fortunes had nosedived. Having left the ministry in Bengal ostensibly because of constant interference by the British governor in the functioning of the government, it had once again become a fringe player in national politics. Its politics of responsive cooperation with the colonial government, adopted to distinguish itself from the Congress, bore scant reward. On the contrary, the early 1940s was the time for the meteoric rise of the Muslim League both in public consciousness and in the eyes of the government. Though the Mahasabha was bitterly opposed to the League's demand for partition, that space for principled opposition was already occupied by Gandhi and the Congress. By 1944, S.P. Mookerjee, who took over the presidency of the Mahasabha, had admitted his limitations, saying that he did not have the cadre to take the views of the Mahasabha to the people.[19] The constitution was a reflection of this reality with the Mahasabha attempting to remain relevant by remaining reasonable. Gone was Savarkar's fiery ideology about India being a nation for Hindus alone; instead, India was to be a nation without a state religion promising equal citizenship to all.

This centrist move was critically a reflection of the growing stature of the Rashtriya Swayamsevak Sangh (RSS). Founded by Keshav Baliram Hedgewar, the RSS was established as a *sangathan* to empower Hindus through physical and martial training. Hedgewar, having started the RSS, continued to remain a secretary in the Hindu Mahasabha, ensuring that the two organizations did not work at cross-purposes.[20] But he was careful to ensure that the RSS stayed aloof from the political programme of the Mahasabha.

The goal of the RSS was avowedly straightforward – to ensure that Hindu youth were trained in self-preservation. Modernizing the traditional concept of the *akhara,* local wrestling clubs, the RSS started *shakhas* where Hindu boys were taught martial skills in a spiritual setting.[21] In its orientation, it was a mass, cadre-based organization that was held together, not by a political programme of swaraj, but rather a cultural programme of reviving Hindu self-confidence and pride. This was a direct product of Hedgewar's admiration of Savarkar's work and disenchantment with Gandhi's methods. As a volunteer with the Congress, Hedgewar was disappointed with Gandhi's non-cooperation technique, which he felt was a sign of Hindu weakness and also with Gandhi's outreach to Muslims supporting the restoration of the *khilafat* in Turkey. Hedgewar was convinced that more assertive methods of protest were needed. Savarkar's *Essentials of Hindutva* provided exactly what he was looking for. With the Mahasabha already focusing on the political representation of Hindus, Hedgewar established the

RSS to focus on their socio-cultural revival. By design, it complemented the Mahasabha perfectly.

Under the surface, however, tensions brewed. Despite the Mahasabha splitting with the Congress in 1928, several RSS members continued to hold dual membership of the Congress. Hedgewar, while aligned with Savarkar's overarching mission of securing Hindusthan for Hindus, was careful not to align the RSS politically.[22] During the Dussehra celebrations of 1932, he claimed that it was for Hindus to decide what rights non-Hindus would have in an independent nation state. This led the Central Provinces government to bar any government servant from becoming a member of the RSS. Quickly, in the Sankranti celebrations in January 1933, he dialled down the rhetoric, saying that the RSS was neither a political nor a communal body and his statements should be viewed accordingly.[23] His equivocation drew him apart somewhat from both Savarkar and B.S. Moonje, another prominent Mahasabha leader at the time. Though this distance never became an open rift, Hedgewar ceased to serve as secretary of the Mahasabha. He also steadfastly kept the RSS out of mainstream politics.

Hedgewar's apolitical orientation had earlier led Moonje to form the Ram Sena on the lines of the RSS. The Ram Sena would ensure military training for Hindu boys, making them agile and capable of self-defence.

Savarkar too started the Hindu Rashtra Dal, ostensibly with similar aims.[24] Neither, however, could match the RSS for its organization and clarity of purpose. In a short span of five years, the RSS grew from 200 branches and 25,000 members in 1936 to 700 branches and 1,50,000 members in 1941.[25] Though most of its membership came from the Maharashtra region, it had slowly started making inroads in north India, particularly Punjab, where the influence of the Muslim League was considerable, opening up space for a direct opponent. With the RSS becoming the predominant representative organization of the Hindu community in several parts of the country and charting its own course, first under Hedgewar and then his successor M.S. Golwalkar, the political clout of the Hindu Mahasabha as the spokesperson for Hindu interests waned further. The RSS showed little interest in constitutional matters generally. It neither endorsed nor opposed the Constitution of the Hindusthan Free State drafted by the Mahasabha. The document was largely ignored, which meant it was dead on arrival.

Not a Real Alternative

The Constitution of the Hindusthan Free State was presented to the working committee of the Hindu Mahasabha in October 1944. The committee appreciated the work by the Gokhale Committee of Poona and proposed that another committee of the Mahasabha with Dadasaheb Kharpande as convener, and S.P. Mookerjee, N.C. Chatterjee, L.B. Bhopatkar, amongst others, as members, study it and present an appropriate resolution before the general body. This resolution to adopt the constitution was moved in December 1944 and duly passed.[26] But despite the constitution being adopted, this was the last time it formed a major part of the discussions at a Hindu Mahasabha session. Needless to say, it rarely featured in the mainstream of Indian national discourse as well.

Bhopatkar, who was acting president of the Mahasabha in 1946, wrote to the Cabinet Mission urging them to adopt the principles of the Constitution of the Hindusthan Free State, specifically because of the need for a strong Union government emphasizing the indivisibility of the Indian nation state.[27] The Cabinet Mission demurred and its ultimate recommendation to constitute three groups of provinces, two of which were Muslim majority, was seen as a 'stab in the back' of Hindus.[28] The Hindusthan Free State would remain a fantasy.

With the Constitution of the Hindusthan Free State receding into oblivion, some of its more innovative recommendations were never seriously considered by the Constituent Assembly.[29] Particularly integral to its scheme was the conception of popular sovereignty. While all constitutions claimed that sovereignty resided in the people, the Constitution of the Hindusthan Free State went a step further to devise practical mechanisms, apart from universal adult franchise, to make such sovereignty count. Three concrete proposals were initiative, referendum, and recall. Using the initiative mechanism, a minimum threshold of voters could come together and initiate a proposal to table a law, an amendment to a law, or a constitutional amendment in the federal legislature. If passed by the legislature, it would become the law of the land, like any other legislation. Referendum carried its ordinary meaning. In case of all non-money bills, the legislators could reserve a matter for direct voting by the people through a referendum. Only if a requisite majority of people directly voted in favour of a bill would that become law. Recall allowed the people to depose an elected legislator in case of non-performance, even before their term was complete. These mechanisms, according to the drafters of the Constitution of the Hindusthan Free State, were needed to give 'people a direct voice in respect of their social economic well-being and political destiny'.[30]

The drafters of the Constitution of India were more cautious. Though they were drafting a republican constitution with all power flowing from the people, they were equally careful to ensure adequate checks and balances on the people themselves: citizens could only exercise their sovereignty through their representatives and their representatives in turn would be checked by an independent judiciary. A range of other mechanisms were also devised to ensure that the power vested in the people's representatives was not abused. This was not simply because the people could not be trusted. Rather, given how novel democracy was in India, people needed time before they could act maturely. At such a nascent stage, there was no room for unchecked powers like referendum, recall, or initiative. In short, direct democracy would come later.

In the Constituent Assembly, S.P. Mookerjee, who might have been expected to press for some of the distinct principles contained in the Constitution of the Hindusthan Free State, did not do so. For Mookerjee, the Constitution of India that the Constituent Assembly had been called on to draft 'was a great responsibility' that had to be exercised 'as a solemn and sacred trust'.[31] Mookerjee remained firm that drafting the Constitution was not a matter for 'different political parties and platforms' but had to be done unanimously. Searching for unanimity, Mookerjee raised those principles from the Constitution of the Hindusthan Free State that were broadly aligned with the thinking of the majority of the members of the Constituent Assembly. He demanded a strong Union government to prevent future secessions, Sanskrit as the national language, and largely supported the vision of the Drafting Committee of a republican constitution based on the principles of liberty, equality, and fraternity.

This underlined a salient truth: the Constitution of the Hindusthan Free State was, in essence, not an alternative to the Constitution of India. One may have imagined that with Savarkar's careful outlining of the ideology of Hindutva, the constitution that had his blessing would also be imbued with Hindutva. But this wasn't the case. Speaking in the Constituent Assembly, Narhar Vishnu Gadgil, a Congressman, noted that between the Constitution of the Hindusthan Free State (and the Socialist constitution[32]) on the one hand and the draft Constitution of India on the other, 'there is agreement on the main features of the Constitution that ought to prevail in this country'.[33] Though there were certainly differences, their basic structure, borrowed as it were from the best that global constitutions had to offer, was the same.

The Constitution of the Hindusthan Free State was, in essence, a document designed to make the Hindu Mahasabha a part of the political mainstream and a responsible national party. This was recognition of the fact that its fortunes had been slipping, both on account of the overwhelming popularity of Gandhi, who had firmly captured the Hindu imagination, and the tenuous relationship with the RSS which was firmly ascendant at the time. This is why, though much shorter than the eventual Constitution of India, its basic principles, were largely analogous. To the extent that there were differences, the Hindu Mahasabha did not have the political support to press those differences effectively. It was a fringe player in national politics at the time and would remain that way for much of independent India's early existence. Hindutva doctrine would flourish outside the constitutional scheme both as a matter of design and politics. Its constitutional face would remain staunchly nationalist and committed to freeing India from the yoke of colonial rule.

SIX

India

Ambedkar did not himself write the Constitution of India. He shared much of the vision of the members of the Constituent Assembly about a constitution that would make India a sovereign, democratic republic. The Constitution is a reflection of that shared vision.

From the forehead of darkness,
Bhim – the child of light
In the womb of the black mother,
Pens the Constitution . . .

– Lok Shahir Sambhaji Bhagat

It must have been preordained.

At the turn of the twentieth century, young Bhim found himself stranded at Masur station in Bombay province with his elder brother and two nephews. None of the bullock cart men would take a family of Mahar children to Koregaon, where Bhim's father worked, even if they were willing to pay the fare. Mahars were untouchables, kept at a distance, physically and metaphorically, by caste Hindus.

One cart man agreed on the condition that the children would pay double the fare, drive the cart themselves and the cart man would walk alongside. Their slow progress meant that they had to halt midway at a village for their meal and rest. Neither the villagers, nor the toll collector, let alone the cart man, gave the children even a sip of water for fear of being polluted. Though the boys had carried plenty of food, in the absence of water, they could not touch it. Hungry, angry, and bitterly thirsty, Bhim reached Koregaon the next morning.[1]

Half a century later, in the Central Hall of Parliament, the people of India, adopted, enacted, and gave to themselves the Constitution of India. 'Irresistible, indomitable, unconquering levelling down tall palms and short poppies'[2] – praises for Dr Bhimrao Ramji Ambedkar and his work as the chairman of the Drafting Committee of the Constitution were overflowing. The president, Rajendra Prasad, was particularly gushing: 'We could never make a decision which was or could be ever so right as when we put him (Ambedkar) on the Drafting Committee and made him its Chairman. He has not only justified his selection but has added lustre to the work which he has done.'[3]

A century later, on the occasion of the fiftieth year of the Republic of India, Lord Bingham, Lord Chief Justice of England and Wales, described the Constitution as 'an enduring monument to the wisdom, erudition and idealism of Dr Ambedkar and all others who framed this remarkable document'.[4] By that time, Ambedkar had, in the popular imagination, become the founding father of the Constitution, its chief architect, its author. Statues had sprung up across the country depicting him in a trademark blue suit, holding a copy of the Constitution in one hand, the other outstretched as if pointing the way ahead to his fellow Indians. A member of Parliament estimated that there were at least 10 lakh (1 million) statues of him across the country, installed mostly by ordinary people.[5] From being denied water as a Mahar child, he was now being remembered, often venerated, at railway stations, bazaars, and village corners. His compelling life story had come full circle. Bhim, the child of destiny, was now Dr Babasaheb Ambedkar, father of the Constitution of India.

Ambedkar's remarkable rise from the depths of social backwardness in colonial India to the heights of public office in an independent nation made him the subject of widespread adulation. For Dalits, as a Marathi folk song described him, he was like a mother, all-protecting and the reason for life itself.[6] Politically, he was the philosophical inspiration for the Bahujan Samaj Party, championing Dalit empowerment, the Republican Party of India, and countless local Dalit activist organizations and ideologues. Over time, he transcended the image of Dalit icon and became a national leader. His birthday, 14 April, is a national holiday. Parties from across the political spectrum, hostile to Ambedkar during his lifetime, now queue up to pay their respects. He has a statue outside the Indian parliament and his quotes are common in speeches of political leaders in all parts of the country.

The centrepiece of this adulation is the Constitution, now widely recognized as his definitive achievement in the establishment of modern India.

Ambedkar's Constitution?

Was Ambedkar solely responsible for drafting the colonial constitution? Any draftsman will know that a text, 395 articles long, with subsections, clauses and sub-clauses, is unlikely to be the work of a single individual. Such a document is usually the product of its time, collectively shaped by the best minds available. Ambedkar himself grasped this instinctively: 'The principles embodied in the Constitution are the views of the present generation or if you think this to be an over-statement, I say they are the views of the members of the Constituent Assembly. Why blame the Drafting Committee for embodying them in the Constitution?'[7]

In absolving the Drafting Committee of blame from unhappy members of the Assembly, Ambedkar was merely restating some hard facts. In January 1947, the Constituent Assembly had adopted the Objectives Resolution. The resolution itself was drafted by Jawaharlal Nehru and based on the views of the Experts Committee appointed by the Congress for this purpose. Ambedkar, not being a member of the Congress, had no role to play in it. When the Objectives Resolution was moved in the Constituent Assembly, Ambedkar's response was equivocal.[8] He critiqued parts of the declaration relating to justice and freedom, saying that they had no mechanisms for enforcement. This appeared to be criticism for the sake of it: one could hardly expect a resolution designed to set the objectives of the Constitution to also set out enforcement mechanisms. If that was the expectation, then the Experts Committee alone could have drafted the entire Constitution, leaving nothing for the rest of the Constituent Assembly to do.

More trenchant was his critique of the federal scheme envisaged in the Objectives Resolution, designed to accommodate the demands of the Muslim League. 'I like a strong united Centre, much stronger than the Centre we had created under the Government of India Act of 1935,'[9] said Ambedkar to cheers in the Assembly. He candidly admitted that the powerful colonial government was to him 'a matter of great admiration and respect and refuge'.[10]

The Objectives Resolution, however, had diluted the strength of the central government considerably. The provinces would be the primary wielders of power, except in certain pan-India matters like defence, foreign affairs, and communications which were assigned to the Union. Critically, all residuary powers – matters which were not expressly spelt out in the Constitution and future areas of legislation – would remain with the provinces. If this portion of the Objectives Resolution had found its way into the Constitution, then the internet today would be regulated by state governments, different banking rules would be prevalent in different states, and states would be at liberty to decide whether income tax should be levied for their residents or not. Ambedkar chafed at this line of thinking – taking power as far away from local leaders was his vision for how India would grow and prosper.

Despite this firm conviction, Ambedkar did not want the Constituent Assembly to take the decision of making India a strong, unitary state in the absence of the Muslim League which was boycotting proceedings. The halfway house of the Constituent Assembly framing a constitution for united India with the representation of significant sections of its population hanging in the balance was unacceptable to him. Either the Muslim League should be won over by reason or let go of. In both cases, the Constitution should not deviate from the strongly centralizing character of the Government of India Act.

His objection, however, didn't elicit much of a response. Sarojini Naidu remarked that though Ambedkar appeared to be bitter during the discussion on the Objectives Resolution and the functioning of the Constituent Assembly itself, she hoped that over time he would become 'an emphatic supporter'.[11] Her olive branch worked, and the Objectives Resolution was unanimously approved.

As the hard work of drafting the text of the Constitution based on the resolution began, the Assembly set up several committees to accomplish this task. The Advisory Committee on Fundamental Rights, Minorities and Tribal and Excluded Areas to recommend a set of fundamental rights including rights of minorities, the Union Constitution Committee and the Provincial Constitution Committee dealing with the structure of the Union and provincial governments respectively, and the Union Powers Committee dealing with Centre–state division of powers, were critical to the ultimate shape the Constitution would take.[12] Ambedkar was a member of the Advisory Committee including its Sub-Committee on Minorities and Sub-Committee on Fundamental Rights, as well as the Union Constitution Committee, besides a number of other committees.[13] His presence was all-pervading, though his influence, at least initially, less so.

His most telling contribution in this committee-driven phase of drafting of the Constitution of India, as described earlier, was the presentation of the draft of proposed fundamental rights titled 'Constitution of the United States of India'. Drafted by Ambedkar on behalf of the All India Scheduled Castes Federation, this was presented to the Sub-Committee on Fundamental Rights, of which he was a member.[14] Given this is the only known set of provisions that he himself drafted, it is as close as one can get to an unadulterated Ambedkarite constitution.[15] Despite this painstakingly prepared draft on fundamental rights being presented to the sub-committee, the draft that formed the basis for their discussion was an alternative draft prepared by K.M. Munshi and worked on further by B.N. Rau.[16] Only two items in Ambedkar's draft were discussed. His suggestion to abolish any privilege or disability arising out of birth, rank, etc. was accepted. Also accepted was another suggestion that untouchability should be abolished and discrimination against any person with regard to the use of wells and tanks be outlawed.

His other suggestions, particularly those that had defined his political career – separate electorates for Scheduled Castes and reserved seats for them in legislatures – were not discussed at all. Yet another set of suggestions relating to making India an economic democracy were not substantively discussed at that stage, but incorporated indirectly. While Ambedkar had suggested making these provisions – such as ownership of key industries by the state and an obligation on every adult citizen to take out a life insurance policy provided by the state – mandatory, the sub-committee's draft included them as a set of non-justiciable, non-enforceable rights that ultimately became the Directive Principles of State Policy.

Despite the sub-committee ignoring the majority of his suggestions, Ambedkar wrote a very brief dissent note. It touched only on two matters – first, Ambedkar believed that Hindustani should be made the national language, not only in the Union, but also the states; second, he said the option of a compulsory military conscription should not be foreclosed.[17] He remained silent on the rejection of his proposals on reservation and separate electorates. He was similarly silent when in the Sub-Committee on Minorities, a provision for separate electorates was shot down. This was out of character for a man for whom dignity for the Depressed Classes was intrinsically intertwined with their right to vote exclusively for their own representatives. So was his nationalistic tone of dissent arguing for Hindustani usage and military conscription. They only made sense in terms of the imminent and sudden change in his role in the Constituent Assembly that happened within three months.

While the various committees of the Assembly were submitting their reports one by one in early 1947, the constitutional adviser B.N. Rau, along with the Constitutional Assembly Secretariat, had the painstaking task of putting these drafts together into a coherent constitution. This was an onerous task: there were twelve committees which had together prepared twenty-two reports. Given the volume of work as well as its significance,

Rajendra Prasad, the president of the Constituent Assembly, acted on an earlier recommendation and set up the Drafting Committee – a super committee headed by Ambedkar to 'scrutinise'[18] the draft prepared by Rau and revise it before presenting it to the Assembly. While scrutinizing sounded innocuous, with the chairmanship of the Drafting Committee, Ambedkar took his first significant step towards prominence in the Assembly, and ultimately recognition as the author of the Constitution itself.

Ambedkar's journey to membership of the Constituent Assembly had not been straightforward. According to the Cabinet Mission Plan, members of the Assembly representing provinces would be elected by members of provincial legislatures. Representatives were divided between Muslims, Sikhs (wherever relevant), and the general category, which included caste Hindus and Scheduled Castes. Members of the Assembly belonging to these communities would exclusively elect their own representatives. The numbers of seats allocated to each province, and within a province to each community were dependent on population. In essence, persons could be elected only if the Congress or the Muslim League supported their candidature.

Ambedkar first tried and failed to be elected from Bombay province. Despite this reversal, Jogendranath

Mandal, Scheduled Caste leader from Bengal and future law minister of Pakistan, lobbied hard to find a way in for him. Mandal, who represented Bengal, sacrificed his seat for Ambedkar.[19] No sooner had this happened than Partition was announced. Seats that had been allocated to Sind and the North-West Frontier Province would now be for membership to the Constituent Assembly of Pakistan, while seats for Punjab, Assam, and Bengal would now be divided between India and Pakistan. Ambedkar's seat was allocated to Pakistan; once again, his prospects of being in the Constituent Assembly seemed bleak.

At that time, Rajendra Prasad made a decisive intervention. In a remarkably candid letter, Prasad, shedding his propriety of being the president of the Assembly, requested B.G. Kher, the Congress chief minister of Bombay, to ensure that Ambedkar, despite being a non-Congress leader, be nominated from his home province.[20] At the same time, Nehru had been angling for renowned British jurist Ivor Jennings to be appointed as chairman of the Drafting Committee.[21] Gandhi would have none of it: he was clear that when there were home-grown constitution experts like Ambedkar, there was no need to look elsewhere.[22]

On 30 August 1947, Ambedkar, now representing Bombay province with the support of the Congress, was made chairman of the Drafting Committee.[23]

The title of the committee was somewhat misleading and has given rise to the impression that the Drafting Committee alone drafted the Constitution. Based on the reports of the several committees that the Assembly had set up, the constitutional adviser B.N. Rau and the Constituent Assembly Secretariat had prepared a basic first draft, as noted above; it consisted of 240 articles and 13 schedules. The task of the Drafting Committee was nonetheless significant. It had to finalize Rau's draft, take it to the Constituent Assembly, amend it on the basis of deliberations there, and seek its final ratification.

Being thrust into the forefront of the drafting process, Ambedkar led the work of the Drafting Committee with dedication and diligence. The Committee had forty-four sittings in seven months to hammer out a consolidated draft that could be presented before the Assembly. While other members were itinerant, Ambedkar remained constant throughout.

During this time, the Drafting Committee took several key calls, albeit not radically altering the structure of the Constitution drafted by Rau. The definition of India was changed to a 'Union of States' from a 'Federation', emphasizing the unity of India and the centralizing bent of the Constitution; 'due process of law' was changed to 'procedure established by law', widening the powers of the state to detain persons; the tenure of the prime minister was increased to five years from four to ensure that the requirements of re-election did not unduly hinder large-scale societal reform. In all these changes, the imprint of Ambedkar, champion of a big state with a powerful Union government, was unmistakable. Yet Ambedkar did not treat the Drafting Committee chairmanship as carte blanche to include all his constitutional ideas that had so far not been consensually agreed upon. No separate electorates were incorporated, provisions on economic democracy remained weak, reservation for Depressed Classes remained limited to seats in legislatures and not in executive government or jobs, as Ambedkar had earlier demanded in his original constitutional formulation.

This was not surprising given that in the Drafting Committee, despite being its chairman, it was not as if it was Ambedkar alone scrutinizing the drafts, striking through old provisions, writing in new ones. As he himself acknowledged, the draft Constitution would not have been possible without the contribution of B.N. Rau and S.N. Mukherjee, a joint secretary in the Constituent Assembly Secretariat, who were present at every meeting alongside Ambedkar. Mukherjee, described by Ambedkar as 'the Chief Draftsman',[24] and his team were the technical drafting experts who dotted the i's and crossed the t's, ensuring that the Constitution that was finally enacted was an error-free, internally consistent document.[25]

As Ambedkar himself acknowledged, 'Without his [Mukherjee's] help, this assembly would have taken many more years to finalise the Constitution.'[26]

Once the draft Constitution had been placed in the public domain for consultation in February 1948, Ambedkar came much more into his own. One of the key tasks of the Drafting Committee was implementing the recommendations of all committees in draft form. One such committee, the Committee on the Chief Commissioner's Provinces, had recommended that citizens residing in certain geographically small areas – Coorg, Ajmer–Merwara, Panth Piploda, the Andaman and Nicobar Islands, and Delhi – should also enjoy responsible government and not be administered directly by the Union as had been the case in colonial India. Specifically for Delhi, it recommended a responsible legislature together with a lieutenant governor appointed by the president to be the final arbiter of differences that may arise.[27] Ambedkar and the Drafting Committee took exception. 'As the capital of India it can hardly be placed under local administration,' he said.[28] Instead, it vested full powers in the president to administer these territories through a lieutenant governor, a governor of a neighbouring state, or a local legislature, as deemed fit. For Ambedkar, local administration in a small territory would be a free pass to prejudice and petty partisan politics. Refusing to be bound by the propriety of his terms of reference as the chairman of the Drafting Committee, he frankly placed his suggestion before the Assembly that Delhi not be granted autonomy and statehood. His view carried the day, despite robust opposition from members from Delhi itself.

Typically, when faced with a difference of opinion on an issue, the president of the Assembly turned to Ambedkar for his view. More often than not, this became the view of the Assembly. K.T. Shah had suggested an amendment to Article 1 of the Constitution saying that differences between various types of states – older British provinces, larger princely states, smaller princely states, Chief Commissioner's Provinces, new, merged states – should be dismantled over a period of ten years.[29] This was proposed so that the Constitution vested all states with similar powers of responsible government and India became a true Union of states. Despite voluble support in the House, Ambedkar would have none of it. After an amendment was proposed and before putting it to vote, the chair almost inevitably turned to Ambedkar, giving him the last word. He dismissed this amendment summarily, simply stating that he opposed it. If this amendment were accepted, the continuing fracas over the governance of Delhi would have become a thing of the past. But Ambedkar thought differently and the Assembly went along with him.

While sometimes it was Ambedkar the ideologue who had the last word, at other times it was Ambedkar, the legal expert. Mohammad Tahir had proposed an amendment to specifically make discrimination criminally punishable. Ambedkar, while agreeing with Tahir, pointed out why that would be superfluous. Untouchability had already been declared to be an offence that would be punishable. Regarding other violations of fundamental rights, Parliament had been vested with the general right in another article, to make such laws as may be necessary to provide for punishments. This was in order to enable Parliament to prescribe uniform penalties across India and not leave any discretion with the states. In this context, yet another specific criminal penalty was unnecessary.[30] His careful parsing of Tahir's amendment led to its withdrawal, something many members did after Ambedkar had spoken.

At the conclusion of the innings of the Constituent Assembly on 26 November 1949, its members had taken the new Indian dominion to a respectable score. Earlier that year, the Dominion of India had played its last match of test cricket, against the West Indies at the Brabourne Stadium in Bombay. Chasing an improbable 361 to win in the fourth innings against the might of the West Indies, Rusi Modi and Lala Amarnath provided a steady foundation. Vijay Hazare came in and crafted a masterful century with support from Vinoo Mankad. Dattatray Phadkar, Shute Banerjee, Hemu Adhikari, and Ghulam Ahmed put up a creditable rearguard action. The match was drawn. Ending at 355 for the loss of 8 wickets, India remained agonizingly short of victory, yet had staved off defeat.

Much of the work of the Constituent Assembly resembled this landmark game. B.N. Rau and Rajendra Prasad had provided a solid opening. Ambedkar had been the star of the middle overs, constructing the innings painstakingly together with K.M. Munshi and his colleagues in the Drafting Committee. Nehru and Patel ensured consensus that took the document over the line, seeing the innings out to a respectable close.

Neither was Ambedkar alone responsible for the text nor was he merely a top dressing to make the Constitution respectable to all sections of society. The Constitution was a collective enterprise of all its framers. It reflected their vision of what the republic needed to get off the ground and to deliver on the promises made in its Preamble. The framers' views were, in turn, a product of the times in which they lived and the established wisdom of constitution drafting. The fact that the Constitution is wholly identified with Ambedkar today has much to do with the fact that the dominant thinking at the time aligned with and found a powerful voice in Ambedkar's writing. He may not have written much of the initial text. But its vision matched his in large part, making him the ideal candidate to shape its contours to give it coherence. It also made for a more compelling story.

New India, Not Quit India

'He could read, he could write, he could walk, he could bathe, and he could rest with a status of equality. Meals at regular hours, eating on a table, cloth and napkin . . . it was a new world.'[31]

With a generous grant from the maharaja of Baroda, Ambedkar enrolled in Columbia University in 1913.[32] He thrived in the atmosphere of equality that the United States afforded him. As he recollected, 'My five years of staying in Europe and America had completely wiped out of my mind any consciousness that I was an untouchable.'[33] America gave him both dignity as a person and freedom as an intellectual. Not being segregated from others, as he was in India, he had the opportunity to immerse himself in the intellectual pleasures Columbia had to offer. He worked hard to make his new-found freedom count. He submitted a thesis on the finances of the East India Company for an MA degree in 1915. He later took admission at the London School of Economics, graduating with a DSc.[34] He went back to Columbia to get a doctorate to round off his academic pursuits.

At Columbia, Ambedkar was known as a diligent student, working day and night at his studies. He refused to be drawn into the Ghadar Party, active at the time in the United States, striving for swaraj for India.[35] Later in England too, he largely steered clear of revolutionary activities. Intuitively, he believed that mere swaraj would not do for minorities in India – they needed a set of rights and express safeguards to ensure equality. With his higher education, he was learning the language that would allow him to articulate these intuitions better.

He found that language in his Columbia professor John Dewey's works.[36] Dewey was the proponent of a theory of 'democratic experimentalism', based on free and equal participation. Rather than viewing democracy as mere voting and aggregation of votes, Dewey saw it as a system of 'associated living, of conjoint communicated experience'.[37] If democracy had to work, it needed 'social endosmosis',[38] the ability for individuals to mingle and communicate with each other freely. This was heavy academic jargon. Ambedkar understood it simply: a real democracy is one where citizens are treated equally and untouchables are not kept at a distance.

Such equality, and consequently fraternity, would not come naturally. It would have to be safeguarded through rights for the less privileged in a constitution and effective methods for enforcing them. This would allow individuals from diverse social classes, rich and poor, upper caste and lower caste, to interact and mingle as equals in workplaces, educational institutions, and legislatures. Out of such equality, democratic society would ensue. That was the simple message of an otherwise dense theoretical work.

From Dewey, Ambedkar made social equality his primary objective. This was distinct from the demand for independence, the goal of the Ghadar Party, the Congress, and the contemporary freedom movement. 'More emphasis ought to have been placed on New India – and less on Quit India,'[39] Ambedkar remarked. Its practical necessity hit home almost as soon as he returned to India in 1918.

Exiting the railway station at Baroda, where he had been summoned back by the maharaja, Ambedkar did not know where to look for a place to stay. Hindu hotels would not take him in because of his untouchable status and the government, which he served, had been procrastinating on his request for official accommodation. Without options, he found an inn for Parsis where he was given lodging after entering a false Parsi name in the register and on payment of a handsome amount. But in a few days, this subterfuge was discovered and a group of angry Parsi men accused him of defiling their inn. He was unceremoniously thrown out.[40]

He approached two friends in Baroda, Hindu and Christian, both of whom pleaded helplessness. One said his servants would refuse to serve an untouchable man, the other claimed that his wife, though a Christian, would never agree to have an untouchable person at home. With nowhere to go, Ambedkar sat in a public garden for a few hours before departing on a train to Bombay. [41] Social endosmosis was no longer theoretical jargon. It was a practical need, to reclaim the dignity of the Depressed Classes.

Armed with the Deweyan language of democratic experimentalism, Ambedkar was quick to put his learnings into action. While giving evidence before the Southborough Committee – which had been appointed by the secretary of state for India and toured the country in 1918 and 1919 to deal with the question of post-war constitutional reforms – Ambedkar argued that the purpose of democracy was not mere representation of opinions but participation of persons. This was why, as a representative of the Depressed Classes, he demanded both reservation of nine seats in the legislature of the Bombay Presidency and separate electorates of only persons belonging to the Depressed Classes to vote for these nine members.[42] Only a combination of the two, crystallized in law, would lead to a chance of equality. Social endosmosis would not happen organically from below, it would have to be specifically mandated from above.

This formed the basis of his view that for the Depressed

Classes, demanding a swaraj constitution with special safeguards comprising reservation of seats and separate electorates was the ideal way forward. Right up to the proceedings of the Constituent Assembly, Ambedkar remained steadfast that only such a constitution would mark a departure from the continuing deprivation experienced by the Depressed Classes, first from caste Hindus, and later the British. In neither case did the Scheduled Castes have basic dignity: caste Hindus denied them access to temples and jobs, and kept them untouchable. Scriptural sanction was claimed as justification. However, even without the historical baggage of scripture, the all-powerful colonial government in Delhi, whose presence was initially welcomed by the Depressed Classes, did little to alleviate their plight. This was not because as a powerful sovereign government whose writ ran across the whole of British India, they could not. Rather, the British chose not to wade into the morass of local politics on a cultural issue where taking any side would create resistance to their rule. The colonial experience convinced Ambedkar that a powerful, independent state alone would not do. Such a state would simply replace colonial rulers with Indians, who would perpetuate pre-existing caste prejudices. Their best chance was a powerful state that was mandated by the Constitution to protect and promote the interests of the Depressed Classes.

Delhi Rule

'I confess I have a partiality for a Unitary form of Government. I think India needs it,'[43] said Ambedkar criticizing the Government of India Act, 1935. For him, an ideally powerful government should not have to deal with the complexities of federal division of powers. That would divide sovereignty, loyalty, and ultimately the ability to act in cases of emergency. 'The existence in the country of one Government which can speak and act in the name of and with the unified will of the whole nation is no doubt the strongest Government that can be had and only a strong Government can be depended upon to act in an emergency.'[44]

But Ambedkar was too astute an observer of political affairs to harbour any ambition of the ideal unitary government being established in independent India. He was always quick to caveat his remarks by adding that 'local autonomy [should not be] inconsistent with central unity'.[45] This was commonsensical – India was the size of a continent, scarcely ever in history had a single sovereign authority ruled over the entire territory. Even during the Raj, a complex system of paramountcy had been developed by which the British ensured their overlordship over innumerable maharajas and maharanis. Geographical and linguistic subnationalism was common. Added to the mix was the religious subnationalism of the Muslim League. The question was no longer about a mythical unitary government: it was about how to create a federation that would not wholly defang the central government.

It was obvious that any federation, no matter how weak, would lead to some degree of provincial autonomy. Ambedkar did not oppose such autonomy; in fact, as a member of the Bombay Legislative Council, he made a presentation to the Simon Commission in 1929 arguing that provinces should have a list of subjects where they could be sovereign.[46] However, this did not mean that the Union would be weakened. The Union should be directly elected by the people, have exclusive jurisdiction on most key subjects, and have the authority to override the province in case it is 'non-functioning' or acting 'in a manner prejudicial to the interests of the country'.[47] Here was the precursor to the emergency provisions in the Constitution of India.

In Ambedkar's view, such overriding powers of the central government in a federation were critical for safeguarding the rights of minorities. The closer the government was to the people, the closer it would be to their prejudices and discrimination against the minorities who live in their midst. Since the Depressed Classes would be a minority in all provinces, Ambedkar put it plainly: 'There must be some authority somewhere, over and above the Provincial Government, which will be in a position to intervene and rescue them from any adverse position in which they may be placed by the Provincial majorities.'[48]

As a child of a Mahar, appealing to the good sense of the representatives of the cart man who would not ferry him and his brothers, and the toll collector who would not give them water, seemed like a mockery of democracy. Yet Ambedkar did not give up on democracy, the need for social endosmosis, and the objective of fraternity that had remained elusive. Instead, that faint hope was invested in a strong central government administered by Indians with guaranteed Depressed Class representation. Only such a government would function without local prejudices, being mandated to do so by a progressive constitution that safeguarded the rights of minorities.

At the Depressed Classes Conference in Nagpur in 1930, Ambedkar laid out his nuanced view on the need for a big, swaraj state with a powerful Union government. He praised European civilization for giving Indians the concepts of 'liberty, equality, fraternity', the language of which became a powerful tool to call out entrenched and discriminatory social customs. Yet, as he said, the British government had only paid lip service to these principles. It inherited a set of discriminatory social arrangements and, though it had all the legal powers to declare them unlawful, chose to perpetuate them 'like the Chinese tailor who, when given an old coat as a pattern, produced with pride an exact replica, rents, patches and all'.[49] That coat would only change with the state having to work according to a swaraj constitution that would protect the Depressed Classes. This would happen when political sovereignty passed from British hands to Indian hands, and in one fell swoop, the Depressed Classes were given a meaningful share in Indian power.

When the time came to demand that share, Ambedkar was categorical that the British should divide power between caste Hindus and the Depressed Classes before leaving, instead of entrusting that decision to the Constituent Assembly. In such an Assembly, Ambedkar felt that caste Hindus would outvote the Depressed Classes, making all promises of future safeguards illusory. In a memorandum submitted to the Cabinet Mission in April 1946, he revealed his disinclination towards any Constituent Assembly of Indians at all. Instead, he submitted that the task of constitution drafting was not as complex as to require an Assembly. Technical questions should be left to a commission headed by a foreign jurist. That commission would be given the task of recommending any changes as may be necessary to the Government of India Act, 1935.[50] For Ambedkar, that Act provided the basic structure of the big state with a strong Union government that independent India needed. Regarding communal questions that might arise, a conference of leaders of different communities, presumably like the Round Table Conferences, ought to be convened. If the leaders could not reach consensus, an Award should be made. Ambedkar's view of the proposed constitution was clear: the Government of India Act was a good enough base draft ensuring a powerful state; any changes could be made by the foreigner-led commission, with prickly communal issues settled mutually.

As provocative as Ambedkar's methods might have sounded, his substantive views resonated with the Constituent Assembly. The Congress had already outlined its view of India as an independent sovereign republic that would ensure not only political freedom for its citizens but also their economic sustenance. Here was Ambedkar, a strident critic of the Congress, who was supporting the Congress' demand of creating a strong and indivisible Union through the Constitution. What added lustre to the exercise was both Ambedkar's erudition and his personal belief that not only for India as a nation, but also for its weakest and most backward minorities, the Constitution would be a charter of hope. Yet for that hope to fructify, there was an elephant in the room that had yet to be fully addressed: what special safeguards would the Depressed Classes have in the Constitution? Ambedkar was clear, but Gandhi had other ideas.

Narsi Mehta's Naysayer

> Gandhi went to the Round Table Conference with a song of the saint Narsi Mehta on his tongue. It would have been better for him and better for his country if he had taken in his arm pit a volume on comparative constitutional law.[51]
>
> – B.R. Ambedkar

Three Round Table Conferences were convened by the British Government to discuss constitutional reforms in India between 1930 and 1932. After the wholesale rejection of the Simon Commission report by Indian leaders, these conferences were a renewed attempt by the colonial government to chart out India's constitutional future in a manner that would generate consensus amongst all parties. Legacy issues, such as the attainment of dominion status vis-à-vis complete independence and the full establishment of responsible government at the Centre without the looming overlordship of the British governor-general, remained thorny. However, with representatives of British India and Indian princely states being in the same tent for the first time in an official capacity, the British hoped that the parties would be able to broker a consensus on power-sharing in a new constitutional set-up.

Ambedkar represented the Depressed Classes at the Round Table Conferences. True to his training, he viewed these gatherings as a political representative of the Depressed Classes' might – an opportunity to press for safeguards for his community of untouchables in any future Constitution of India. But Mahatma Gandhi had other ideas. For him, untouchability was the 'shame . . . of orthodox Hinduism'.[52] He was simply unwilling to countenance any political safeguards for untouchable persons. It was a 'blot', which for Gandhi had to be dealt with by Hindu social reformers spreading the message of unity. This was a matter neither for state intervention nor for political negotiation. '*Vaishnava jana to tene kahiye je peed paraayi jaane re*' (One who is a Vaishnava knows the pain of others) – unity would ensue from the collective singing of Narsi Mehta's hymn, not from the doctrines of comparative constitutional law.

To forge this unity, with uncharacteristic immodesty, Gandhi claimed in the Second Round Table Conference, which was the first and only one that the Congress attended, that if a referendum were to be held amongst Depressed Class persons, he would 'top the poll' and be elected their representative. He questioned Ambedkar's claim to represent all Depressed Class persons, blamed him for putting his own bitterness ahead of his community's travails, and, ultimately, castigated him for not knowing India and the basics of Indian society.[53] Unsurprisingly, the Round Table Conferences made no headway in resolving the communal question of power-sharing in a new constitution, let alone formulating its basic framework.

With the failure of the conferences, Prime Minister Ramsay MacDonald announced the Communal Award to settle the question of how communities would be represented in legislatures. To resolve the stalemate relating to the Depressed Classes, the Award gave members of the Depressed Classes two votes: one in the general category as part of a joint electorate, the other in a special category of seats reserved for twenty years for Depressed Class candidates to be elected exclusively by a Depressed Class electorate. Seventy-one such seats were identified for reservation, where Depressed Classes were demographically most numerous.[54] This was along the lines of what Ambedkar had demanded.

Gandhi categorically rejected the Award. This was expected. When, during the Second Round Table Conference, the Depressed Classes, Anglo-Indians, and Indian Christians had proposed a pact that would give them separate electorates to vote for their own candidates, Gandhi had accused them of 'sit[ting] by the carcass, and they have performed the laudable feat of dissecting that carcass'.[55] As with his unwavering resistance to cutting up the Indian electorate into slices then, Gandhi took a principled stand on the Communal Award: 'But I hold that separate electorates is harmful for them and for Hinduism, whatever it may be from the purely political standpoint.'[56]

Ambedkar was dismissive of Gandhi's so-called principles. Gandhi could not be principally averse to separate electorates, he believed, since he had no hesitation in accepting them for Muslims. The Muslim League and the Congress had a long-standing pact entered into in Lucknow in 1916 by which Muslims would vote for their own representatives in provincial assemblies through an exclusively Muslim electorate. This pre-dated Gandhi, but had been generally accepted by successive Congress leaders as an acceptable price for cooperation by the Muslim League in the struggle for freedom. When it came to the Depressed Classes, Gandhi sang from a different hymn sheet.

This, Ambedkar believed, was because Gandhi did not genuinely consider persons belonging to the Depressed Classes as equals of caste Hindus. As evidence, he pointed to the Congress under Gandhi's overall leadership continuing to fund separate schools and wells for Depressed Classes. Ambedkar was convinced that Gandhi had only one objective: 'Mr. Gandhi wanted the Untouchables to live under his providence and that of the Congress . . .'[57] The struggle was no longer merely political, it was intensely personal.

On 18 August 1932, Gandhi wrote to Ramsay MacDonald from Yerwada Central Jail, objecting to the Communal Award: 'I have to resist your decision with my life. The only way I can do so is by declaring a perpetual fast unto death from food of any kind save water with or without salt and soda.'[58] MacDonald was uncompromising and stated plainly that the only method by which the Award could be modified was if the Depressed Classes could be convinced to give up their demands. Ambedkar was in an uncomfortable dilemma: 'Mr. Gandhi's life . . . was in my hands.'[59]

Under considerable pressure, Ambedkar and Gandhi agreed on a set of points to alter the Communal Award. The Poona Pact, as the agreement commonly came to be described, was an elaborate scheme for reservation of seats for Depressed Classes in the central and provincial legislatures out of the seats allotted for Hindus, in lieu of separate electorates. For reserved seats, only Depressed Class persons in those constituencies would elect four persons from whom one would, in turn, be elected by the general electorate. This two-tier voting system would operate in place of separate electorates for the Depressed Classes, and would continue for ten years, unless terminated earlier.[60] Thus, though a certain number of seats would be reserved for candidates belonging to the Depressed Classes, the candidate would be elected by a joint electorate of not only members of the Depressed Classes, but also caste Hindus. Reservation of seats was an acceptable price Gandhi was willing to pay to stave off the 'poison' of separate electorates. With the Poona Pact having been agreed, he broke his fast on the seventh day.[61]

Despite this détente, the constitutional fault line between Gandhi and Ambedkar was clear and apparent. Gandhi believed that the 'constitutional engineering'[62] of the British was not the solution to the problem of untouchability; it lay in changing hearts and minds of caste Hindus. Those hearts would get hardened if separate electorates were created, keeping the Depressed Classes walled off. For Ambedkar on the other hand, any self-government was better than good government. He intuitively grasped Gandhi's logic that real change would only come when the social institution of caste was attacked. But such an attack could not come from within a society that was entirely adherent to it. Instead, it needed an external stimulus that could be provided by a constitution. Political rights for the Depressed Classes were not ends in themselves, they were means to acquire strength that would in turn lead to a more equal society.

The Poona Pact had managed to paper over this philosophical disagreement, but not for long. When, building on this interim détente, Gandhi asked Ambedkar to write a message for the first issue of *Harijan*, Gandhi's new weekly publication for the uplift of the Depressed Classes, Ambedkar refused. Instead, he provided a caustic message for publication:

> The outcaste is a bye-product of the caste system. There will be outcastes as long as there are castes. Nothing can emancipate the outcaste except the destruction of the caste system. Nothing can help to save Hindus and ensure their survival in the coming struggle except the purging of the Hindu faith of this odious and vicious dogma.[63]

It was evident that while a political compromise had been reached, little had bridged the trust deficit between them. The results of the 1937 elections contested on the terms of the Poona Pact only widened this deficit. It resulted in 151 representatives of the Depressed Classes being elected, but the majority of them were from the Congress party.[64] Though the candidate who received the most votes in the primary elections amongst Depressed Class voters did not belong to the Congress, in the secondary vote by the general electorate, the majority of Congressmen emerged victorious. This was bound to happen, as Depressed Class voters were outnumbered by caste Hindus in most constituencies with reserved seats.[65]

Ambedkar felt he had been played. The Poona Pact had meant Depressed Class representatives would now have to court the Congress in order to get elected. As a result, the Depressed Classes were only 'marking time' under the Government of India Act.[66]

Despite Ambedkar making several petitions to the colonial government, delivering some rousing speeches, writing powerfully and evocatively on the continuing plight of the Depressed Classes, and demanding a return to separate electorates, that ship appeared to have sailed. Reservation of seats had become an accepted principle of representation. Added to that, reservation in government jobs to ensure adequate representation had also gained acceptability as a special provision that could be made by the state. Both of these were part of the draft circulated by B.N. Rau to the members of the Constituent Assembly.[67] No separate electorates for Depressed Classes made it to any official draft of the Constitution of India.

Ambedkar's persistent advocacy had meant that reservations, unheard of in Western constitutions to which drafters primarily turned for inspiration, became a fundamental component of India's imminent constitution. The perpetuation of untouchability meant that there was no question of simply trusting Hindus to reform themselves. This fundamental lack of trust could only be bridged through political rights safeguarded in a mutually acceptable constitution. The logic of reservation to safeguard the political rights of the Scheduled Castes, as Depressed Classes were now called by the Constitution, was Ambedkar's chief original contribution, a product of his lived experiences, his dogged political advocacy, his vision of a more equal India.

This constitutionalization of the caste question meant that the question of dignity for the Scheduled Castes in independent India primarily became a matter of political negotiation. Integration was expected to flow from the acquisition of material entitlements of government jobs and the ability to politically advocate for one's cause in legislatures. This led to, as the perceptive social commentator D.R. Nagaraj remarked, the Dalit movement evoking 'fear and resentment' amongst caste Hindus.[68] No longer were they integral members of the 'rich and complex spiritual universe' of Hindus; rather, they had become the confrontational 'other' who had to be grudgingly accommodated.

Ambedkar might have been optimistic when he accepted reservation of seats for a period of ten years as sufficient to begin with. It was no surprise that almost as soon as the Constitution began functioning, Ambedkar restated something he had known all along: mere constitutionalization of the caste question, including the constitutional outlawing of untouchability, would not alone be sufficient. Untouchability, a social phenomenon that dated back millennia, could not simply be legislated away by the stroke of a pen. If the Constitution had given anyone or Ambedkar himself this hope, he now said that he was 'quite prepared to be the first person to burn it [the Constitution] out. I do not want it. It does not suit anybody.'[69]

For a man who had played such a critical role in drafting the Constitution and ensuring optimal safeguards for the Scheduled Castes, this was a remarkable statement. It was testament to the limitation of what a constitution, drafted following the basic structure of the colonial government, could achieve. It could somewhat restrain governments, not compel them to act; invest citizens with rights, not provide forums where they could understand each other better; set up courts as enforcers, not local mediators who could amicably settle disputes; declare India to be striving for liberty, equality, and fraternity, yet not be able to make citizens more sympathetic to the plight of fellow countrymen. This is perhaps why once the Constitution started functioning, Ambedkar had mixed feelings. While defending it as 'a beautiful document', he was quick to disavow his own role in drafting it. 'I was a hack. What I was asked to do, I did much against my will.'[70]

Ambedkar was acutely aware that the Constitution could not set down the roots of a society based on liberty, equality, and fraternity, and repudiate caste, overnight. It could be legislated in a moment, but its fruits would take considerable time to emerge. In this, he and Gandhi were on the same page: the Constitution would nourish the soil of India in which it was planted but would also have to be nourished by it. Like a mango tree could not grow in a desert, neither could a constitution establish a casteless society simply by providing reservation for the Scheduled Castes in legislatures and jobs for ten years. Neither Ambedkar nor Gandhi lived long enough after the Constitution came into existence – Gandhi died before 1950, Ambedkar in 1956 – to see the fruits of their labours. But in death they were united in a way that they scarcely were in life – in their realization that constitutions don't change countries, countries create constitutions that are conducive to their time. The colonial constitution was the Constitution of India circa 1950. Narsi Mehta's 'Vaishnava jana to', on the other hand, remains timeless.

EPILOGUE

Inflection Point

Irrespective of political affiliation, it is time to start thinking about new constitutional ideas for India.

On 26 January 2020, at Shaheen Bagh in New Delhi, thousands of citizens collectively read the Preamble to the Constitution as a mark of solidarity and non-violent protest. They were protesting against the Citizenship Amendment Act, 2019 and the National Register of Citizens. The Citizenship Amendment Act had simplified the process of acquiring citizenship for Hindus, Buddhists, Jains, Parsis, Christians, and Sikhs from Bangladesh, Pakistan, and Afghanistan. The National Register of Citizens would provide a conclusive list of those whom the Government of India considered citizens of India. Their combined message was clear: Muslims were unwelcome in India. The constitutional ideal of fraternity was being challenged.

A few kilometres away at India Gate, India was celebrating its seventy-first Republic Day. As usual, a procession of decorated floats took part in a spectacular parade down Rajpath (now Kartavya Path). Classical Odissi dancers shared the spotlight with Rajasthani folk artists, Kashmiri musicians played the *rabab* as their counterparts from Assam performed the *bhortal nritya.* In his 'Mann ki Baat' broadcast to the nation, Prime Minister Narendra Modi spoke about how refugees from the Bru-Reang community, displaced from their homes in Mizoram in the remote north-east of the country owing to ethnic tensions, had been successfully brought back home. 'Considering everyone as its own and living with the spirit of togetherness is embedded in the ethos of this holy land,' he declared.[1] Fraternity, from the geographical extremities of the country to the heart of the national capital, seemed alive and well.

The government and those protesting against it clearly had different notions of who counted as belonging to the fraternity of the Indian nation state. Both claimed the mantle of diversity, but differently. The Constitution provided the site for this contest, as it had for similar contests over the last seventy years. But the resolution of this contest will not simply depend on the words in the text; after all, the words of the Constitution can be amended, and have been, a whopping 105 times. Any resolution would be guided by its spirit, depending on how far such spirit had permeated into the hearts and minds of citizens, and whether, according to them, that spirit too now needs to change.

How this resolution will play out is not obvious. But it is

clear that we are at an inflection point with the old giving way to the new. Liberalization of markets has replaced the constitutional creed of state socialism as the dominant economic ideology of our times; universal poverty alleviation programmes are taking precedence over identity-based reservation in jobs and education; parties advocating Hindutva are no longer fringe elements, they are centre stage in national and state politics. It will be no surprise if the Constitution follows suit and reflects some of these changes.

But the Constitution, itself a creature of continuity, has time and again showed its staying power. That became most visible in a photograph captured in the town of Bareilly on 30 March 2020 during the first wave of the COVID-19 pandemic. Approximately fifty migrant labourers walking home were made to sit on their haunches by the roadside. They were then sprayed with disinfectant to rid them of the virus. The indignity of being made to squat in public and then being forcibly made to bathe in disinfectant captured in one image the reality of the colonial constitution. The state stood above with a chemical spray. Citizens sat below, with bowed heads, awaiting their fate. Much had changed in seventy years, but equally, very little had. The Constitution had continued a colonial state in 1950. It had shown its true colours in Bareilly in 2020. Seven decades on, and before the question creeps up on us unknowingly, it is time to ask the hard question: does India need a new constitution?

This is not a call to draft a new constitution today. We live in polarized times and any constitution that emerges out of such a time is unlikely to be long-lasting. But it is a call to think more deeply about the Constitution rather than merely extolling its virtues in a rhetorical fashion or criticizing it unthinkingly. The Constitution creates a towering state that stifles individual initiative. It creates big governments that diminish the role of local communities. It gives citizens fundamental rights but hedges them with a slew of restrictions. At the same time, it spells out a clear vision of a more equal, secular, democratic India with free and fair elections based on universal adult franchise. If India is to prosper, it needs to embrace some of what the Constitution has to offer: the promise of freedom, communal harmony, and equality. Equally, it has to reject some other bits: preventive detention, rights without meaningful duties, a colonial state which over time has become a rent-seeking one. India today needs an honest conversation about its colonial constitution and whether it is ready to chart its own constitutional course. The time for banal homilies is over.

APPENDIX

A Timeline of Events

25 May 1909

- The Indian Councils Act is enacted, formally introducing the idea of separate electorates by giving this benefit to the Muslim community.

23 December 1919

- The Government of India Act, 1919, is enacted into law, continuing the idea of separate electorates for Muslims and extending it to Sikhs, Indian Christians, Anglo-Indians, and Europeans.

August 1928

- The Motilal Nehru Committee submits its report, a document widely regarded as the first constitutional document for Indians by Indians. It has a chapter on fundamental rights, a parliamentary form of government, division of powers between the Centre and provinces, a unified judiciary with a new Supreme Court above the

High Courts, and the concept of reservations for uplift of certain groups.

7 June 1930

- The Simon Commission submits its report recommending 'responsible self-government' in provinces, but also clarifying that the lynchpin of provincial governance will continue to be the unelected governors.

November 1930–January 1931; September–December 1931; November–December 1932

- Following the wholesale rejection of the Simon Commission report by Indian leaders, the British government convenes three Round Table Conferences to chart out India's constitutional future.

16 August 1932

- After the lack of consensus at the Round Table Conferences, the Communal Award is announced by British prime minister Ramsay MacDonald recognizing not only Muslims, Christians, and Sikhs, but also the Depressed Classes of Hindus as minorities who will vote for their own representatives through separate electorates.

24 September 1932

- After M.K. Gandhi's staunch opposition to the Communal Award, the Poona Pact is concluded between him and B.R. Ambedkar deciding that caste Hindus and members of the Depressed Classes will vote in joint electorates in the elections to fill the seats reserved for the Depressed Classes.

1 April 1935

- The Government of India Act, 1935, is enacted into law.

12–14 April 1936

- At the Lucknow session of the Congress, Jawaharlal Nehru decries the Government of India Act, 1935, as a 'new charter of slavery'.

February 1937

- The first elections are held under the Government of India Act, 1935. Congress sweeps into power in six provinces: Madras, Bihar, Orissa, Central Provinces, United Provinces, and Bombay.
- The Muslim League captures only a quarter of the seats reserved for Muslims and the Congress takes less than 10 per cent. Most Muslim seats are won by regional Muslim parties.

1938

- A charter is proclaimed in the princely state of Aundh (in present-day Maharashtra) establishing and deepening the democratic ties between the ruler and his subjects.

October–December 1939

- Congress ministries across all provinces resign en masse in protest against Britain making India a part of the war effort without consulting any Indian leaders. Section 93 of the Government of India Act, 1935, is invoked in some provinces imposing Governor's Rule, and coalition ministries are formed in some provinces.

1939

- The Constitution of Aundh comes into force; it is based entirely on the Gandhian conception of village republics.

March 1942

- As the Second World War rages on, Sir Stafford Cripps presents his offer proposing to grant India dominion status with the right to frame its own constitution, establish a Constituent Assembly for this purpose consisting of representatives from provinces and states, but also recognizing the right of provinces or states to opt out of the Constitution if they felt that their interests had not been safeguarded.

8 August 1942

- Quit India resolution is adopted by the All India Congress Committee demanding immediate end of British rule in India. It states that a provisional government of independent India will establish a Constituent Assembly to draft a constitution acceptable to all.
- The resolution clarified that the Constitution would be 'a federal one, with the largest measure of autonomy for the federating units, and with residuary powers vesting in these units'.
- Quit India movement is launched, and the top brass of the Congress (anyone who had subscribed to the resolution) is arrested.

December 1942

- Tej Bahadur Sapru takes the initiative to resolve the deadlock by setting up a meeting at Allahabad. This is attended by C. Rajagopalachari (who has not subscribed to the resolution and is therefore free), as well as spokesmen of the Hindu Mahasabha, the Christian Conference, the Trade Union Congress, the Liberal Federation, the Akali Party, and the Federation of Indian Chambers of Commerce.

- After two days of discussions, it is apparent that without the Congress and the Muslim League present in full force, no firm course of action can be agreed upon.
- Sapru sends a cable to Prime Minister Churchill suggesting, inter alia, the following measures:
  - Till the end of the war, conversion of the Central Executive Council into a full-fledged national government, consisting entirely of representatives from all parties (primarily the Muslim League and Congress) in charge of all portfolios and accountable only to the Crown (the legislature could not dismiss the national government).
  - Restoration of popular governments in the provinces, which were now being ruled by the governors by invoking Section 93 of the Government of India Act, 1935 (proclamation issued by governor in case of failure of constitutional machinery in a province).
- None of these suggestions are accepted.

April 1944

- Rajagopalachari prepares a proposal for settlement between the Congress and the Muslim League in consultation with Gandhi (who is still incarcerated) and sends this to M.A. Jinnah. This proposal states:

- The Muslim League will accept the demand for India's independence and cooperate with the Congress in setting up an interim government in the transitional period following independence.
- After the Second World War is over, a commission will be appointed to demarcate contiguous districts in the north-west and east of India where Muslims are in absolute majority. A plebiscite in these areas will then determine whether the inhabitants will remain part of a united India or form a sovereign state of their own. Upon separation, the two states will enter into a mutual agreement for cooperation in essential areas such as defence, commerce, communications, etc.

July 1944

- Sapru again takes the initiative and meets Gandhi after his release from prison, along with Rajagopalachari and Bhulabhai Desai (a Congress leader from Bombay).
- Gandhi approves of the suggestion that lawyers of note should draft a memorandum explaining the reasonableness of the measures proposed by Sapru in his cable.

24 September 1944

- Gandhi writes to Jinnah clarifying certain aspects of the Rajagopalachari formula:
  - The commission should be one approved by both the Congress and the Muslim League.
  - The plebiscites are to be based on adult franchise or some equivalent method.

- The agreement/treaty between the two states should contain provisions not only for defence, commerce, communications, foreign affairs, customs, etc. but also for the protection of minorities.
- While full cooperation is desirable, the Muslim League will be free to not participate in any direct action which the Congress might choose to resort to.

October 1944

- Jinnah responds to Gandhi, rejecting most of his proposals. He explains that a plebiscite cannot be conducted: Muslims constitute a separate nation, and so they cannot be asked whether they want to separate or not. He also confirms that a treaty between India and Pakistan for cooperation in the areas proposed by Gandhi is not possible as these subjects are the lifeblood of any sovereign state.

November 1944

- Sapru again takes the initiative and requests Gandhi to convene an all-parties national convention. Gandhi refuses. The two then agree to set up a committee to study the situation and propose a potential solution. It is also agreed that the members will not be members of either the Congress, the Muslim League, or any of the recognized parties, and that they will be persons who have not taken any position after the breakdown of the Gandhi–Jinnah talks in October.
- Sapru sets up such a committee consisting of himself and twenty-nine other individuals distinguished in public affairs.

January 1945

- The Bhulabhai Desai–Liaqat Ali Plan is formulated in near secrecy, with neither person supplying information about the negotiations with their superiors. The plan states:
  - The Congress and the Muslim League will join an interim government at the Centre in the form of a central executive as envisaged under the Government of India Act, 1935. The composition of this government is to be an equal number of persons nominated by the two parties who need not be members of the central legislature, minority representatives, and the governor-general.
  - Though the interim government is to function in accordance with the Government of India Act, 1935, the cabinet cannot resort to any of the reserve powers available to the governor-general or viceroy under that Act if they cannot get their way with the legislative assembly.
  - Some way should be found to persuade the viceroy to invite the Muslim League and the Congress to join an interim government to be formed along the lines agreed upon in this plan.
- After its leak in the press, Liaqat Ali Khan denies having ever formally agreed to the plan. Jinnah and the rest of the Muslim League ridicule it. The Congress does not formally subscribe to the plan either, and Desai sees himself sidelined in the Congress leadership as a result of the failure of this pact. He is not offered a chance to contest a seat in the Constituent Assembly.

March 1945

- Viceroy Wavell realizes that Germany is likely to be defeated soon, and with the end of the war, the promise of dominion status to India will have to be kept. He departs for London for a meeting with the British government to discuss his idea: a conference of all the important leaders in the country with the British government to discuss the formation of a transitional government under the Government of India Act, 1935. The executive is to consist of equal numbers of Hindus and Muslims, as well as one representative each of the Scheduled Castes and Sikhs, in addition to the viceroy as the commander-in-chief. The task of this government will be to proceed with the war against Japan, and carry on the administration of India till a new constitution can be drafted, and to determine the composition of the Constituent Assembly which will draft such a document.
- Crucially, the Indian ministers in the executive will be given critical portfolios such as external affairs, which had hitherto been the exclusive domain of the viceroy.
- The British government broadly accepts this idea.

April 1945

- The Sapru Committee submits a 345-page report containing valuable commentary on the current political and constitutional moment in India. Compiled by Sapru, M.R. Jayakar, N.G. Ayyangar, and Jagdish Prasad, its contents are as follows:

- **Two nation theory**
  - The two-nation theory is rejected as an 'outrage justified neither by history nor by political expediency'.
- **Interim arrangement**
  - India is to be made a dominion. To achieve this, popular governments are to be re-established in all provinces. In establishing such governments, even if a party enjoys an outright majority, it will have to include persons in its government who enjoy the confidence of all major parties in the assembly.
  - A national government is to be formed at the central level. This is to be achieved through one of two options:
    i) An amendment to the Government of India Act, 1935, to ensure that the governor-general in council, which till then had consisted of British officials appointed by the British government, will consist only of Indian members commanding the confidence of the central legislature (except the commander-in-chief who will continue to be an ex officio member of the council in charge of war operations), OR
    ii) By finally operationalizing Chapters II and III of Part II of the Government of India Act, 1935, which established the federal executive and federal legislature respectively.
- **Permanent arrangement**
  - A Constituent Assembly is to be set up with a total membership of 160. This Assembly is to be elected

by the provincial legislatures through proportional representation.
  - This Assembly will set up a constitution from which it will not be possible for individual provinces and states to opt out – in direct contravention of the Cripps offer.
- This report does not lead to any concrete solution. This is primarily because the wholesale rejection of the two-nation theory means that the Muslim League does not consider the report to be a serious constitutional document. Further, parity in numbers between non-Scheduled Caste Hindus and Muslims in the Assembly's membership (the report allotted fifty-one seats to both communities) irks many Hindus.

14 June 1945

- Secretary of State for India Amery makes a statement in the House of Commons stating:
  - The Cripps offer of 1942 is still alive in its entirety and it is still hoped that the Congress and the Muslim League will come to a consensus about the permanent future form of government in India.
  - The executive council is to be reconstituted and the viceroy will make his selection for nomination of members of this council from among Indian leaders, in such a proportion so as to give equal representation to Hindus and Muslims, and proportionate representation to the other communities.

- To pursue this plan, the viceroy will invite prominent leaders of all parties to advise him.

14 June 1945

- On the same day, Viceroy Wavell delivers a broadcast talk explaining who he intends to invite to advise him. A body is to be set up consisting of:
  - All those holding office as premiers in provincial governments or who last held office before Section 93 was imposed.
  - Leaders of the Congress and the Muslim League in the Central Assembly and Council of State – the two houses of legislature at the central level – and also leaders of the Nationalist Party and European representatives in the Central Assembly.
  - Gandhi and Jinnah as the recognized leaders of the two main parties.
  - Rao Bahadur N. Sivaraj to represent the Scheduled Castes and Tara Singh to represent the Sikhs.
- Wavell's plan is met with a massive backlash from the Hindu Mahasabha owing to his insistence on treating 250 million Hindus and 90 million Muslims on an equal footing by giving them an equal number of seats in the executive council. It is also opposed by the Muslim League – which feels that only it has the right to nominate all the Muslim members of the council. This claim is opposed by all other parties.
- Wavell declares that Jinnah's plan is unreasonable, but without the support of the Muslim League, it will not be

possible to proceed with the plan. Accordingly, he declares his plan a failure and seeks some time to reconsider.

July 1945

- The Labour Party sweeps to power in Britain. The new prime minister, Attlee, seeks to reopen negotiations with the Indian leaders. He has the advantage of having had a discussion with B.N. Rau – who went on to become the constitutional adviser and who had shared with Attlee Nehru's views on the subject of drafting a constitution: that fresh elections would have to be conducted under the Government of India Act, 1935, to constitute an interim central government, and the strength of the Constituent Assembly should be fixed at 300 or 400 to account for all interests, but the task of drafting would have to be entrusted to a small committee to be appointed by the Assembly. To safeguard the interests of minorities, an upper house could be formed in the central legislature based on indirect elections from provinces. On the question of partition, Nehru favoured the idea of half-cantons in Switzerland, i.e. the creation of half-provinces with a certain degree of autonomy in, inter alia, cultural matters.

September 1945

- Wavell announces that elections are to be held to reconstitute all provincial legislatures as well as the central legislature.

January 1946

- Elections are held. The Muslim League wins all seats reserved for Muslims in the central legislature as well as most seats reserved at the provincial level, locking in its status as the pre-eminent representative of the Muslim community in India.

19 February 1946

- A statement is made by the Labour government in the British parliament proclaiming that a special mission of cabinet ministers (Secretary of State for India Pethick-Lawrence, president of the Board of Trade, Cripps, and First Lord of the Admiralty Alexander) will find a way to set up an interim government agreeable to all.

24 March 1946

- The Cabinet Mission arrives in India and begins discussions with all parties and leaders.

10 April 1946

- Jinnah convenes a meeting with all persons elected to legislatures on a Muslim League ticket. A resolution is passed demanding that the sovereign state of Pakistan be carved out consisting of six provinces: Bengal, Assam, Punjab, the North-West Frontier Province, Sind, and Baluchistan. The resolution also demands the setting up of two Constituent Assemblies for each independent state.
- The Congress opposes this resolution. Within a united India, it is prepared to provide the maximum possible local autonomy to provincial governments – with the

central government only responsible for critical subjects such as defence, communications, foreign affairs, etc. The Congress also suggests that a list of optional subjects could be created over which the provinces could grant legislative and executive competence to the Centre.

16 May 1946

- The Cabinet Mission releases its plan. It states that a separate state of Pakistan will not solve the communal minority problem and will also be antithetical to the interests of the large number of Hindus and other minorities living in the provinces sought to be carved out. It also provides a host of administrative, logistical, military, economic, and strategic arguments against partition.
- The Congress's views are also rejected as disadvantageous. Instead, the following is proposed:
- **Interim arrangement**
  - An interim government is to be formed consisting of Indian members chosen by the British government in consultation with Indian parties. These members are to be handed all portfolios currently handled by the viceroy.
  - Since the Government of India Act, 1935, would have to be continued in the interim period (in the absence of an alternative) it would not be possible to make this interim government directly responsible to the central legislature.

- **Permanent arrangement**
  - There will be a single Union government exercising powers over a very short list of enlisted subjects with all residuary powers vesting in provinces.
  - The Union is to have a legislature and an executive.
  - Provinces should be free to form groups with their executives and legislatures, and each group can then determine the provincial subjects which are to be included within the fold of the provincial constitutions.
  - Every ten years, through a majority vote, a provincial assembly can call for reconsideration of the terms of the Constitution.
  - The Constituent Assembly is to be elected by leveraging the recent elections held to constitute the provincial legislatures under the Government of India Act, 1935. Each province is to be allotted a fixed number of seats in proportion to its population (in the ratio of one to a million). This number would then be divided between the main communities in each province in proportion to their population. The representatives of each community are to be elected only by members of the legislative assemblies belonging to those communities. The elections would be conducted through proportional representation by single transferable vote.
  - All provinces are to be divided into three sections: Section A consising of Madras, Bombay, Uttar Pradesh, Bihar, Central Provinces, and Orissa, Section B of Punjab, the North-West Frontier Province, and Sind,

and Section C of Bengal and Assam. The five centrally administered Chief Commissioner's Provinces – Panth Piploda, Andaman and Nicobar Islands, Coorg, Ajmer–Merwara and Delhi – are to be distributed among sections A and B.

- After being elected, the Constituent Assembly will first elect a chairman from amongst its members. Administrative committees will then be set up by election amongst members. Then, the Advisory Committee on Fundamental Rights, Minorities, and Tribal and Excluded Areas will be elected by the Constituent Assembly. Next, the Constituent Assembly will determine which powers are to be reserved for the Union in accordance with the Cabinet Mission Plan. Finally, the Constituent Assembly will divide itself into sections A–C to draft the provincial constitutions and also determine whether group constitutions will be necessary. Then, the three sections will reassemble to draft the Union Constitution.
- Any proposal which seeks to alter the basic features of the Constitution or raises any major communal issues will require the votes of the majority of representatives present and voting of both Hindu and Muslim communities.
- Princely states will also be given seats in the Assembly (not exceeding ninety-three), but in the preliminary stage they will be represented by a negotiating committee.

- The Congress instantly opposes the plan as the representatives of Sind and Baluchistan would be grouped with Punjab and those of Assam would be grouped with Bengal – and owing to the Muslim majority in the groups, the rights of other communities in those provinces would not be safeguarded in the provincial constitutions. It seeks a clarification from the Cabinet Mission as to whether these provinces, upon resolutions being passed by their legislative assemblies, could decline to be a part of the sections to which they had been assigned.
- The Muslim League also appears to be opposed to the plan as the creation of an independent Pakistan is still its desired goal.
- Eventually, both parties reluctantly accept the Cabinet Mission Plan with reservations.

6 June 1946

- The Council of the Muslim League issues a resolution declaring that though it has accepted the Cabinet Mission Plan, its ultimate goal is still the creation of an independent Pakistan.
- The reason the League accepts the plan is that it sees the idea of Pakistan inherent in the plan since the six Muslim provinces had been placed in sections B and C. The League feels that the plan contains an implicit right of each province or group of provinces to secede from the Union.

16 June 1946

- The viceroy publishes a list of fourteen members for the proposed executive council including six from the Congress (all non-Muslims) and five from the Muslim League.

25 June 1946

- With its attempts to include a Muslim Congressman in the executive council failing, the Congress adopts a resolution declaring its intention to join the Constituent Assembly but rejecting the list published by the viceroy.
- Around this time, the Muslim League adopts a resolution expressing its willingness to join the interim government.

26 June 1946

- The Cabinet Mission announces that the formation of the interim government is to be postponed in light of the difference of opinion between the two parties.

28 June 1946

- Jinnah writes a letter to the viceroy arguing that if the formation of the interim government is to be postponed, the elections to the Constituent Assembly should also be similarly postponed; according to him, both form part of a single integral scheme as per the Cabinet Mission Plan. With one being put on hold, the acceptance of the other by the League appears illogical to Jinnah.
- The viceroy refuses to accept this demand. Even though the formation of the interim government can be postponed, this is not the case for the establishment of the Constituent Assembly – as the core objective of the Cabinet Mission is to ensure that a constitution is framed without any delay.

10 July 1946

- Nehru speaks in a press conference making several controversial remarks about the grouping of provinces. He suggests that provinces in Section A would not agree to the grouping; the North-West Frontier Province in Section B would not agree, making that group collapse; and Assam would similarly not agree to a grouping with Bengal, making Section C collapse as well. He insinuates that if things are allowed to play out, grouping would not prove to be a concern as it would be extinguished as a concept after the Constituent Assembly had commenced its work.
- It has been surmised that Nehru used the word 'group' when in fact he meant 'section'. Notably, the Cabinet Mission Plan had clarified that there was a difference between the representatives of the provinces being divided into three sections – which was compulsory – and sitting in groups – which was anyway voluntary to begin with. It is thus clear that Nehru was referring to Assam not sitting with Bengal in Section C.

27–29 July 1946

- The Muslim League adopts a series of resolutions:
  - Criticizing the Congress for failing to accept the Cabinet Mission Plan in its unadulterated form and also the viceroy for failing to set up the interim government and trying to appease the Congress.
  - Withdrawing its acceptance of the Cabinet Mission Plan.

- Calling all Muslims to resort to action to achieve an independent Pakistan by observing a direct action day on 16 August 1946.

July 1946

- Congress sets up an Experts Committee consisting of Nehru (chairman), Asaf Ali, K.M. Munshi, N.G. Ayyangar, K.T. Shah, D.R. Gadgil, Humayun Kabir, and K. Santhanam (members) to put together material for the Constituent Assembly.
- This committee conducts two meetings (20–22 July and 15–17 August). The procedure it evolves is as follows:
  - The Constituent Assembly elects a temporary chairman from amongst its members, preferably by agreement between the Congress and the Muslim League. A resolution is then adopted electing a permanent chairman. Administrative committees are then set up by election amongst members. Then, the Fundamental Rights Committee (with a membership of forty-five, not all of whom are members of the Constituent Assembly) is elected by the Constituent Assembly. The Constituent Assembly then defines its objectives in the form of a resolution (a draft of which has been prepared by this committee). Next, the Constituent Assembly determines which powers are to be reserved for the Union in accordance with the Cabinet Mission Plan. Finally, the Constituent Assembly divides itself into sections to draft the provincial constitution.

July 1946

- Elections to the Constituent Assembly from the provincial legislatures are completed: of the 210 seats reserved for the general category, the Congress wins 199, and of the seventy-eight seats reserved for Muslims, the Muslim League wins seventy-three. Including some of the Sikh representatives and the representatives of three of the Chief Commissioner's Provinces who were also Congressmen, the Congress tally in the Constituent Assembly stands at 208 – a little more than half the total membership of the Assembly.

12 August 1946

- Realizing it is unwise to delay the transfer of power any longer, Viceroy Wavell issues a press communique declaring that he has invited the president of the Congress, Nehru, to form the interim government and that Nehru has accepted this proposal.
- At Wavell's behest, Nehru tries to convince Jinnah to join the government but to no avail.

2 September 1946

- Interim government consisting entirely of Congress nominees assumes office.
- Convening of the Constituent Assembly is postponed to December to give the Muslim League a chance to join the interim government.

September 1946

- Jinnah meets Rau, now the constitutional adviser, and asks him ten pointed questions on the procedure to be adopted by the Constituent Assembly. Rau writes back explaining that if the end goal is the same, i.e. drafting a constitution for India, there should be no issues in agreeing upon the means.

26 October 1946

- Wavell personally intercedes with Jinnah and convinces him to nominate five members from the Muslim League to the interim government without any further stipulations or conditions.
- Wavell also convinces Nehru that if the Muslim League is to join the interim government, it will only be on the condition that they would accept the Cabinet Mission Plan and also join the Constituent Assembly.
- Based on this understanding, the Muslim League nominees are sworn into the interim government.

Early November 1946

- Jinnah writes to Wavell repeating the charge that the Congress has not fully accepted the Cabinet Mission Plan. Specifically, he points out that the Congress has refused to accept that the provinces are unable to break away from their assigned sections. According to the Congress, this right is inherent in the Cabinet Mission Plan. This is not the Muslim League's reading of the plan, and admittedly, this is not what the plan said.
- Jinnah demands that if the Constituent Assembly is to function at all, it is necessary for Wavell to not only get the Congress to explicitly agree to the text of the Cabinet Mission Plan and all of its proposals, but also

devise ways to ensure that the Congress does not break its promise. In light of the communal riots which have broken out, Jinnah demands that Wavell immediately call off the proposed meeting of the Constituent Assembly in December.

20 November 1946

- Wavell issues an invitation to all members of the Constituent Assembly to attend its first meeting on 9 December.

26 November 1946

- Wavell issues an invitation to Nehru, Jinnah, Liaqat Ali Khan, and Baldev Singh on behalf of the British government for discussions in London to reach a consensus.

Late November 1946

- Rau writes a letter to Nehru casting aspersions on the legitimacy of the upcoming proceedings in the Constituent Assembly in the absence of the Muslim League. His argument is that since the Cabinet Mission Plan did not prescribe any quorum for the functioning of the Constituent Assembly (either as a collective or as sections), the default rule is that the majority of the membership would be required to transact business (Rau borrowed this rule from company law). In the absence of the Muslim League, this will not be possible in sections B and C. He points out that the Muslim League might make this point in the upcoming meetings in London and also decide to ask that a reference be made to the Federal

Court for an advisory opinion under the Government of India Act, 1935.

- On the other hand, K.M. Munshi writes a letter to Nehru arguing that the Constituent Assembly can function legitimately without the Muslim League by relying on global practices of Constituent Assemblies in the USA, Australia, etc.

Early December 1946

- Meetings are held in London to resolve the impasse between the Muslim League and the Congress, but to no avail.

6 December 1946

- The British prime minister Clement Attlee issues a statement clarifying that the Congress's interpretation of the Cabinet Mission Plan (i.e. that provinces can choose to break away from their sections or groups) is incorrect. All business would be transacted in a section through a simple majority of those present and voting in the section as a whole, and not the representatives of an individual province. Based on legal advice taken, the prime minister confirms this as the original intention of the Cabinet Mission Plan.
- Accordingly, Attlee urges the Congress to accept this view, so that the Muslim League, which has a strong objection to the notion that provinces could break away from their sections, can reconsider their decision to stay out of the Constituent Assembly.
- If despite this reassurance of the legal position the

Congress is not convinced, Attlee urges the Constituent Assembly to make a reference to the Federal Court as soon as possible.

9 December 1946

- The Constituent Assembly commences its first sitting. Rajendra Prasad is elected chairman (subsequently designated president).

13 December 1946

- Nehru moves the Objectives Resolution, which is met with an immediate backlash from the Muslim League outside the Constituent Assembly on the grounds that crucial decisions pertaining to constitutional design were sought to be taken by the Constituent Assembly in a 'packed' house in the absence of the Muslim League.

22 December 1946

- The Congress Working Committee adopts a resolution objecting to the British prime minister's statement dated 6 December on the grounds that it is not simply a question of legal procedure which turns on a reading of the Cabinet Mission Plan, but a much larger question of provincial autonomy.
- A reference to the Federal Court is of no use, since the British government will not be bound by the verdict, and the Muslim League will refuse to comply with an unfavourable verdict.

23 December 1946

- The Constituent Assembly completes its first sitting.

- After six days of discussion, the Constituent Assembly decides to postpone its consideration to the next meeting. The president explains that this is being done so that the Constituent Assembly has the advantage of the views of the Muslim League.
- Not much is achieved in light of the resolution dated 22 December.

23 December 1946

- Pursuant to the report submitted by the Committee on the Rules of Procedure set up by the Constituent Assembly, the Constituent Assembly formally adopts the Rules of Procedure. These rules provide that the Constituent Assembly is to sit in sections in accordance with the Cabinet Mission Plan to decide whether a group constitution is to be drafted for the provinces included in each section, and if so, what subjects are to be covered in such a constitution. The rules also provide that each section will have absolute freedom to frame its own rules of procedure, provided they do not conflict with those of the Union Assembly or with any decision taken by the Advisory Committee on Fundamental Rights, Minorities, and Tribal and Excluded Areas.

6 January 1947

- The Congress adopts a conciliatory resolution, stating that in the interests of framing a constitution for independent India without undue delay, the Congress will agree to accept the British interpretation of the Cabinet Mission Plan (which aligns with that of the Muslim league) – i.e.

that the representatives from the provinces would sit in their assigned sections, with no right to break away – subject to a total lack of interference by one province in the affairs of another.

22 January 1947

- The Constituent Assembly adopts the Objectives Resolution, which is met with a sharp and immediate backlash from the Muslim League.

31 January 1947

- The Muslim League finally decides it will not be part of the Constituent Assembly.
- It adopts a resolution demanding that the Constituent Assembly be dissolved immediately as the Congress has violated its mandate by passing the Objectives Resolution. Since the Congress has not accepted the 'correct' view on the sections and the grouping, the Cabinet Mission has failed, according to the League, and it would not participate in the Constituent Assembly.

1 February 1947

- Wavell informs the Congress that it is now in a position to demand the resignation of the League's members from the Constituent Assembly. However, he also clarifies that according to him, it is best to run the interim government with the League in coalition rather than in opposition.
- The Congress disagrees with this. According to them, if Wavell is prepared to remove the League from the Constituent Assembly, he should also remove the League nominees from the interim government. If he fails to

secure their withdrawal, the Congress members would themselves resign.

20 February 1947

- Concerned that a potential withdrawal by the Congress from the interim government would further delay the transfer of power, the British decide to act. Prime Minister Attlee announces that British rule in India will end by June 1948, and that power would be handed over to some form of responsible and democratically elected government.
- Critically, Attlee clarifies that if by June 1948 the Constitution that is ready is not one made by a body which effectively represents all provinces and regions, then power will have to be handed over to the central government for most regions, but to the provincial governments in those areas not properly represented in the Constituent Assembly.

Late February 1947

- Rau writes a note to the president of the Constituent Assembly explaining the need to have a provisional constitution ready before June 1948 so that power can be transferred without undue delay.

8 March 1947

- The Congress makes a desperate effort to ensure that the League joins the Constituent Assembly. It adopts a resolution declaring that the Connstitution developed by the Constituent Assembly would only be enforced on those provinces which accept it.

- In this resolution, it also concedes that in light of the worsening situation, the division of Bengal and Punjab along communal lines will have to be considered. (Jinnah was strictly against partitioning Bengal and Punjab with only a portion going to Pakistan – he wanted both provinces to be a part of Pakistan.)

17 March 1947

- Rau circulates a questionnaire on the salient features of the soon to be formulated Constitution to all members of provincial legislatures and the central legislature as well as the members of the Constituent Assembly. Questions are asked on the Union and provincial constitutions, but none on the group constitutions, as the sections had not determined their necessity yet.

30 April 1947

- Rau shares a questionnaire with members of the Union and provincial constitution committees set up by the Constituent Assembly. He receives responses from only one out of twelve members and seven out of twenty-one members respectively.
- Based on the responses and his own views, Rau frames an independent memorandum and detailed draft of the Union constitution which is submitted to the Union Constitution Committee, as well as an independent memorandum on the provincial constitution which is submitted to the Provincial Constitution Committee.

3 June 1947

- As a result of the large-scale communal riots which have erupted, the Muslim League's sharp reaction to the Objectives Resolution, and its sustained failure to participate in the Constituent Assembly, the newly appointed Viceroy Mountbatten is convinced that the situation cannot be helped and that he must hasten the transfer of power to prevent it from worsening any further.
- Accordingly, he unveils his plan to partition British India into two independent states:
  - The approach favoured by the Congress, i.e. giving only a portion of Bengal and Punjab to Pakistan, is chosen.
  - The provincial legislatures of Bengal and Punjab (sans the European members) will meet in two parts, one representing Muslim-majority districts and the other the rest of the province. Each part will vote on the question of carving up the province: if either votes with a simple majority in favour, then the province will be carved up.
  - The parts can then individually decide which country to join. If the two parts decided to stay united, then all members can meet to decide which country to join.
- This plan is accepted by the Congress.

10 June 1947

- The Muslim League adopts a resolution stating that though it cannot agree in principle to the division of Bengal and Punjab, it is willing to accept Mountbatten's plan as a whole.

8 July 1947

- The India Independence Act is passed by the British parliament, carving out the eastern and western parts of Bengal and Punjab respectively, as well as the provinces of Sind, the North-West Frontier Province, British Baluchistan, and Sylhet from the jurisdiction of the Indian Constituent Assembly and transferring them to Pakistan.
- With the passage of this Act, all conditions and restrictions contained in the Cabinet Mission Plan abate.

July–August 1947

- The Constituent Assembly considers the following:
  - The report of the Union Constitution Committee.
  - The second report of the Union Powers Committee (after the first one submitted in April 1947 becomes irrelevant owing to the imminent partition of India).
  - The report of the Advisory Committee on Fundamental Rights on directive principles .
  - The supplementary report of the Advisory Committee on Fundamental Rights on the subject of fundamental rights.
  - The report of the Advisory Committee on Fundamental Rights on the subject of minority rights.
  - The report of the Committee on the Functions of the Constituent Assembly under the Independence Act (appointed to report on the assumption of the dual charge by the Constituent Assembly as the Constituent Assembly and the legislature for the Indian dominion).

  - The report of the Sub-committees on Tribal and Excluded Areas.
  - The second report of the Advisory Committee on Fundamental Rights on the subject of minority rights.
- The Constituent Assembly appoints the Committee on Chief Commissioner's Provinces.
- The Constituent Assembly adopts a resolution appointing the Drafting Committee to scrutinize the draft to be prepared by the constitutional adviser based on the decisions already taken by the Constituent Assembly as well as all necessary ancillary matters.
- The Constituent Assembly is adjourned (the Constituent Assembly meets next in January 1948 for procedural matters, and then only in November 1948 to consider the draft prepared by the Drafting Committee).
- The Sub-committees on Tribal and Excluded Areas submit their reports to the Advisory Committee on Fundamental Rights which agrees with the recommendations, and passes the reports on to the Drafting Committee with a suggestion to draft suitable clauses to incorporate the recommendations of the sub-committees.

September–October 1947

- Rau and the Secretariat of the Constituent Assembly together prepare the first draft and submit it to the Drafting Committee, which commences its scrutiny and revision of the draft.

October 1947–February 1948

- The Drafting Committee revises Rau's draft.

February 1948

- The Drafting Committee finalizes its first revision of Rau's draft and submits it to the Constituent Assembly. This draft is circulated widely for comments from members of the Constituent Assembly, the central executive, the provincial legislatures and executives, federal and provincial courts, and the public at large.

October 1948

- The Drafting Committee meets to consider the comments that have been submitted. It is decided that the Drafting Committee will submit to the Constituent Assembly the version finalized in February 1948. The comments exercise was not futile, as those comments which the Drafting Committee agreed with are presented as motions of amendment sponsored by the Drafting Committee before the Constituent Assembly.

November 1948

- The draft is presented before the Constituent Assembly.
- A clause-by-clause discussion in the Constituent Assembly commences (which goes on till October 1949).

July 1949

- The Drafting Committee holds a conference with representatives from the provincial and federal levels to discuss the legislative, administrative, and financial relationship between the Centre and the states.

October 1949

- The Constituent Assembly completes its clause-by-clause discussion.

- The Drafting Committee begins incorporation of all amendments adopted by the Constituent Assembly as well as any consequential or necessary changes.
- The Drafting Committee as well as other members give notice of certain other amendments.

November 1949

- The Constituent Assembly considers the revised draft along with the newly proposed amendments.
- The motion to adopt the Constitution as settled by the Constituent Assembly is introduced and adopted.

26 January 1950

- The Constitution of India comes into force.

Notes

Prologue: Vaishnava Jana To

1. Neelima Shukla-Bhatt, *Narasinha Mehta of Gujarat: A Legacy of Bhakti in Songs and Stories* (Oxford University Press 2014), 90.
2. K.R. Narayanan, '"Law and Judiciary" (Speech on the occasion of the Golden Jubilee Celebrations of the Supreme Court of India, New Delhi, 28 January 2000)', available on krnarayanan.in.
3. Lord Bingham of Cornhill, Lord Chief Justice of England and Wales, '"Law Day Lecture" (Speech on the occasion of the Golden Jubilee Celebrations of the Supreme Court of India, New Delhi, 26 November 1999)', *SCC*, Vol. 1 (2000): 29.
4. B.R. Ambedkar, Constituent Assembly Debates, Vol. VII, 4 November 1948.
5. Granville Austin, *The Indian Constitution: Cornerstone of a Nation* (Clarendon Press 1966), xi–xiii.
6. *SCC*, Vol. 4 (1973): 225.
7. *K.S. Puttaswamy v Union of India*, *SCC*, Vol. 10 (2017): 1.

8. Madhav Khosla, *India's Founding Moment: The Constitution of a Most Surprising Democracy* (Harvard University Press 2020).
9. Gautam Bhatia, *The Transformative Constitution: A Radical Biography in Nine Acts* (HarperCollins India 2019).
10. M.N. Roy drafted the 'Constitution of Free India: A Draft' in 1944. In this draft, all economic property was to be collectively owned, the right to social security would be guaranteed, and elected committees of citizens – 'People's Committees' – would have the power to initiate laws, demand referendums, and recall representatives. M.N. Roy, *Constitution of Free India: A Draft* (Radical Democratic Party 1944); Niraja Gopal Jayal, *Citizenship and Its Discontents: An Indian History* (Harvard University Press 2013), 143–44.
11. The Socialist Party of India prepared the 'Draft Constitution of the Indian Republic' in 1948, featuring a foreword by Jayaprakash Narayan, the freedom fighter and political activist. This draft granted similar fundamental rights to citizens, such as the right to freedom and equality and further granted economic rights, empowering the state to regulate all private property and economic enterprises, the right to which was guaranteed only to the extent that it would be consistent with public interests. Socialist Party of India, *Draft Constitution of Indian Republic* (1948); Niraja Gopal Jayal, *Citizenship and Its Discontents: An Indian History* (Harvard University Press 2013), 143–44.
12. Kengal Hanumanthaiah, Constituent Assembly Debates, Vol. XI, 17 November 1949.

ONE: Mangu's Angst, Macaulay's Pride

1. '*Naya Kanoon*' [New Constitution or New Law] was a short story written by Saadat Hasan Manto in 1937.
2. B. Shiva Rao (ed.), *The Framing of India's Constitution: A Study* (Indian Institute of Public Administration 1967), 93–106.
3. B. Shiva Rao (ed.), *The Framing of India's Constitution: Select Documents,* Vol. I (Indian Institute of Public Administration 1967), 287–310.
4. B. Shiva Rao (ed.), *The Framing of India's Constitution: A Study* (Indian Institute of Public Administration 1967), 93–106.
5. B. Shiva Rao (ed.), *The Framing of India's Constitution: Select Documents,* Vol. I (Indian Institute of Public Administration 1967), 287–310.
6. B.R. Ambedkar, Constituent Assembly Debates, Vol. VII, 4 November 1948.
7. Government of India Act, 1935, enacting formula.
8. Ornit Shani, *How India Became Democratic: Citizenship and the Making of the Universal Franchise* (Cambridge University Press 2017), 3.
9. Two provisions in the Government of India Act stand out as notable exceptions: Section 275, which prohibited disqualification on the basis of sex in being appointed to the civil services, a civil post, and certain other posts notified by the governor-general, the governor of a province, or the secretary of state; and Section 298, which prohibited discrimination on the basis only of religion, place of birth,

descent, colour, or any of them in being appointed to an office under the crown in India, or from holding or disposing of property or carrying on any occupation, trade, business, or profession in British India.

10. *Selected Works of Jawaharlal Nehru*, Series 1, Vol. 7 (Jawaharlal Nehru Memorial Fund 1988), 183.
11. All India Congress Committee, *Report of the 49th Session of the Indian National Congress, Held at Lucknow, in April 1936* (General Secretary, All India Congress Committee, 1936), 49.
12. Annual Register Office, *The Indian Annual Register: July to December 1936*, Vol. II, 234.
13. Peter Heehs, *India's Freedom Struggle, 1857–1947: A Short History* (Oxford University Press 1988), 125.
14. Arvind Elangovan, *Norms and Politics: Sir Benegal Narsing Rau in the Making of the Indian Constitution, 1935–50* (Oxford University Press 2019), 45–46.
15. B. Shiva Rao (ed.), *The Framing of India's Constitution: Select Documents*, Vol. II (Indian Institute of Public Administration 1967), 433–51.
16. W.W.J., 'The Indian Elections – 1946', *The World Today*, Vol. 2, no. 4 (Royal Institute of International Affairs, Chatham House, April 1946).
17. The India (Provisional Constitution) Order, 1947 (No. GGO 14, 14 August 1947).
18. B.L. Mitter participated in only one meeting of the Drafting Committee. B. Shiva Rao (ed.), *The Framing of India's Constitution: Select Documents*, Vol. III (Indian Institute of Public Administration 1967). N. Madhava Rao was appointed as a member of the Drafting Committee to fill the vacancy

left by Mitter. B. Shiva Rao (ed.), *The Framing of India's Constitution: Select Documents*, Vol. III (Indian Institute of Public Administration 1967), 315.

19. D.P. Khaitan died in 1948 and was replaced by T.T. Krishnamachari, who was the only non-lawyer to serve on the Drafting Committee.
20. B. Shiva Rao (ed.), 'Ambedkar's Memorandum and Draft Articles on the Rights of States and Minorities', *The Framing of India's Constitution: Select Documents*, Vol. II (Indian Institute of Public Administration 1967), 84.
21. B. Shiva Rao (ed.), 'Ambedkar's Memorandum and Draft Articles on the Rights of States and Minorities', *The Framing of India's Constitution: Select Documents*, Vol. II (Indian Institute of Public Administration 1967), 84.
22. B. Shiva Rao (ed.), 'Article II, Section II, Ambedkar's Memorandum and Draft Articles on the Rights of States and Minorities', *The Framing of India's Constitution: Select Documents*, Vol. II (Indian Institute of Public Administration 1967), 88–90.
23. B. Shiva Rao (ed.), *The Framing of India's Constitution: Select Documents*, Vol. II (Indian Institute of Public Administration 1967), 100–01.
24. B. Shiva Rao (ed.), 'Article II, Section IV, State and Minorities: What Are Their Rights and How to Secure Them in the Constitution of Free India', *The Framing of India's Constitution: Select Documents*, Vol. II (Indian Institute of Public Administration 1967), 93–96.
25. B.R. Ambedkar, Constituent Assembly Debates, Vol. VII, 4 November 1948.

26. BR. Ambedkar, Constituent Assembly Debates, Vol. VII, 4 November 1948.
27. B.R. Ambedkar, Constituent Assembly Debates, Vol. VII, 4 November 1948.
28. Hasrat Mohani, Constituent Assembly Debates, Vol. VII, 4 November 1948.
29. Radha Kumud Mookerji, *Local Government in Ancient India* (Oxford: Clarendon Press 1919).
30. Mohd. Tahir, Constituent Assembly Debates, Vol. IV, 28 July 1947.
31. Naziruddin Ahmad, Constituent Assembly Debates, Vol. IV, 28 July 1947.
32. Raj Bahadur, Constituent Assembly Debates, Vol. VII, 9 November 1948.
33. N.G. Ranga, Constituent Assembly Debates, Vol. VII, 9 November 1948.
34. Bipan Chandra et al., *India's Struggle for Independence: 1857–1947* (Penguin, reprinted edition 2016) 365.
35. Damodar Swarup Seth, Constituent Assembly Debates, Vol. VII, 10 December 1948.
36. Lokanath Misra said, 'I therefore submit that unless the manner of the Constitution of this second Chamber is changed and we are in a position to accept something which will be purely Indian based on Indian culture of deep, all-pervasive view and on Indian sentiment and temperament based and nurtured on our traditions which alone can have a sobering influence, the creation of an upper house by itself will have no influence on the House of the People.' Constituent Assembly Debates, Vol. VII, 3 January 1949.

37. Constituent Assembly Debates, Vol. VII, 3 January 1949.
38. Thomas Macaulay, House of Commons Debates, Vol. 19, Col. 536, 10 July 1833.

TWO: The Everything State

1. Second Part, The Constitution of the German Reich, 1919 (Reichgesetzblatt I, 383, Translation of Document 2050 – PS, Office of US Chief of Counsel); Chapter X, 1936 Constitution of the Union of Soviet Socialist Republics (Fifth Impression, Russia Today Society, June 1942).
2. Constitution of Ireland, 1937, Article 45.
3. B. Shiva Rao (ed.), *The Framing of India's Constitution: Select Documents*, Vol. II (Indian Institute of Public Administration 1967), 33–35.
4. B.N. Rau, 'Notes on Fundamental Rights' (2 September 1946), in B. Shiva Rao (ed.), *The Framing of India's Constitution: Select Documents*, Vol. II (Indian Institute of Public Administration 1967), 34.
5. Constitution of Ireland, 1937, Article 45.
6. *Dr Babasaheb Ambedkar: Books and Writings*, Vol. 1 (Dr Ambedkar Foundation, Ministry of Social Justice and Empowerment, Government of India 2020), 409–10.
7. B. Shiva Rao (ed.), *The Framing of India's Constitution: Select Documents*, Vol. II (Indian Institute of Public Administration 1967), 153–54.
8. B. Shiva Rao (ed.), *The Framing of India's Constitution: Select Documents*, Vol. II (Indian Institute of Public Administration 1967), 46.

9. B. Shiva Rao (ed.), *The Framing of India's Constitution: Select Documents*, Vol. II (Indian Institute of Public Administration 1967), 192.
10. B. Shiva Rao (ed.), *The Framing of India's Constitution: Select Documents*, Vol. II (Indian Institute of Public Administration 1967), 146–47.
11. B. Shiva Rao (ed.), *The Framing of India's Constitution: Select Documents*, Vol. II (Indian Institute of Public Administration 1967), 33–36.
12. B. Shiva Rao (ed.), *The Framing of India's Constitution: Select Documents*, Vol. II (Indian Institute of Public Administration 1967), 294–99, 304–05.
13. B. Shiva Rao (ed.), *The Framing of India's Constitution: Select Documents*, Vol. II (Indian Institute of Public Administration 1967), 138.
14. B. Shiva Rao (ed.), *The Framing of India's Constitution: Select Documents*, Vol. II (Indian Institute of Public Administration 1967), 178.
15. B. Shiva Rao (ed.), *The Framing of India's Constitution: Select Documents*, Vol. II (Indian Institute of Public Administration 1967), 291.
16. B. Shiva Rao (ed.), *The Framing of India's Constitution: Select Documents*, Vol. II (Indian Institute of Public Administration 1967), 189.
17. B. Shiva Rao (ed.), *The Framing of India's Constitution: Select Documents*, Vol. II (Indian Institute of Public Administration 1967), 304–05.
18. B. Shiva Rao (ed.), *The Framing of India's Constitution: Select Documents*, Vol. III (Indian Institute of Public Administration 1967), 199.

19. In his travels to the United States, Justice Frankfurter had stated that individual rights should be subject to the general welfare. Justice Learned Hand, the tenth judge of the US Supreme Court, said that the distinction between fundamental rights and directive principles should be done away with by making fundamental rights non-justiciable as well. B. Shiva Rao (ed.), *The Framing of India's Constitution: Select Documents*, Vol. III (Indian Institute of Public Administration 1967), 218.
20. B. Shiva Rao (ed.), *The Framing of India's Constitution: Select Documents*, Vol. III (Indian Institute of Public Administration 1967), 527.
21. T.T. Krishnamachari, Constituent Assembly Debates, Vol. VII, 24 November 1948.
22. *Collected Works of Mahatma Gandhi*, Vol. 83 (Gandhi Sevagram Ashram 1981), 113.
23. Mahavir Tyagi, Constituent Assembly Debates, Vol. VII, 9 November 1948.
24. Jaipal Singh, Constituent Assembly Debates, Vol. VII, 24 November 1948.
25. B.H. Khardekar, Constituent Assembly Debates, Vol. VII, 24 November 1948.
26. K. Santhanam, Constituent Assembly Debates, Vol. VII, 22 November 1948.
27. B.R. Ambedkar, Constituent Assembly Debates, Vol. VII, 4 November 1948.
28. Jabudana Sahaya, Constituent Assembly Debates, Vol. VII, 22 November 1948.
29. T.T. Krishnamachari, Constituent Assembly Debates, Vol. VII, 24 November 1948.

30. Somnath Lahiri, Constituent Assembly Debates, Vol. III, 29 April 1947.
31. Annual Register Office, *The Indian Annual Register: July to December 1929*, Vol. II.
32. Annual Register Office, *The Indian Annual Register: January to June 1930*, Vol. I, 334.
33. *Collected Works of Mahatma Gandhi*, Vol. 4, (Gandhi Sevagram Ashram), 346.
34. *Collected Works of Mahatma Gandhi*, Vol. 4, 454.
35. *Collected Works of Mahatma Gandhi*, Vol. 48, 351–52.
36. *Collected Works of Mahatma Gandhi*, Vol. 48, 351.
37. B. Shiva Rao (ed.), *The Framing of India's Constitution: Select Documents*, Vol. III (Indian Institute of Public Administration 1967), 613.
38. B. Das, Constituent Assembly Debates, Vol. IX, 5 August 1949.
39. Rajendra Prasad, Constituent Assembly Debates, Vol. IX, 5 August 1949.
40. Naziruddin Ahmad, Constituent Assembly Debates, Vol. IX, 5 August 1949.
41. B.R. Ambedkar, Constituent Assembly Debates, Vol. VII, 9 December 1948.
42. B. Shiva Rao (ed.), *The Framing of India's Constitution: Select Documents*, Vol. III (Indian Institute of Public Administration 1967), 67–69.
43. B. Shiva Rao (ed.), *The Framing of India's Constitution: Select Documents*, Vol. II (Indian Institute of Public Administration 1967), 80.
44. Somnath Lahiri, Constituent Assembly Debates, Vol. I, 29 April, 1947.

45. Jawaharlal Nehru, Constituent Assembly Debates, Vol. I, 13 December 1946.
46. Jawaharlal Nehru, Constituent Assembly Debates, Vol. I, 13 December 1946.
47. Jawaharlal Nehru, Constituent Assembly Debates, Vol. I, 13 December 1946.
48. William Vincent, Proceedings of the Indian Legislative Council, Vol. 57, Book No. 2, 6 February 1919, 451.
49. *Collected Works of Mahatma Gandhi*, Vol. 15, 354.
50. *Collected Works of Mahatma Gandhi*, Vol. 15, 375.
51. B.R. Ambedkar, Constituent Assembly Debates, Vol. IX, 15 September 1949.
52. Granville Austin, *The Indian Constitution: Cornerstone of a Nation* (Clarendon Press 1966), 44.
53. Draft Article 15A mandated the production of arrested persons before a magistrate within twenty-four hours of the arrest, required the acquiescence of the magistrate to extend the arrest beyond that period, and provided that no person could be placed in preventive detention for a period beyond three months unless an advisory board opines otherwise, or the preventive detention is under an Act of Parliament.
54. Chimanlal Chakkubhai Shah, Constituent Assembly Debates, Vol. VII, 6 December 1948; Rohan J. Alva, *Liberty After Freedom: A History of Article 21, Due Process and the Constitution of India* (HarperCollins 2022), 5–7.
55. Mahavir Tyagi, Constituent Assembly Debates, Vol. IX, 16 September 1949.
56. Parliamentary Debates, Volume II, 25 February 1950, 874–927.

THREE: New Delhi Darbar

1. Sachchidananda Sinha, Constituent Assembly Debates, Vol. I, 9 December 1946.
2. Sachchidananda Sinha, Constituent Assembly Debates, Vol. I, 9 December 1946.
3. Maurice Gwyer and A. Appadorai, *Speeches and Documents on the Indian Constitution, 1921–47*, Vol. II (Oxford University Press 1957), 618–21.
4. Indian Statutory Commission, *Report of the Indian Statutory Commission, Volume II: Recommendations* (1930), 48–49.
5. Joint Committee on Indian Constitutional Reform, *Report of the Joint Select Committee on Indian Constitutional Reforms*, Vol. I (1934), 43–44.
6. Bureau of Public Information, Government of India, *Speeches and Statements by the Marquess of Linlithgow: 1936–1943* (1945), 228.
7. Clement Attlee, House of Commons Debates, Vol. 357, Col. 1082, 6 February 1940.
8. Thomas Macaulay, House of Commons Debates, Vol. 19, Col. 504, 10 July 1833.
9. John Barnes and David Nicholson, *The Empire at Bay: The Leo Amery Diaries, 1929–1945* (Hutchinson 1988), 48.
10. Other emergency powers, at a time of war or a threat to the nation's financial stability, were also discussed and drafted, eventually becoming Article 352 and Article 360 of the Constitution of India. These are not within the scope of this chapter. For more, see Abhishek Manu Singhvi and

Khagesh Gautam, *The Law of Emergency Powers: Comparative Common Law Perspectives* (Springer 2020).

11. The other members initially appointed to the Union Powers Committee were Sarat Chandra Bose, Dr Pattabhi Sitaramayya, Jairamdas Daulatram, Biswanath Das, Bakshi Tek Chand, and M.R. Masani. In April 1947, two representatives from the princely states were added: V.T. Krishnamachari and B.L. Mitter.
12. C. Rajagopalachari, Constituent Assembly Debates, Vol. II, 25 January 1947.
13. On the very same day, Rajagopalachari addressed the Assembly on the need to proceed at pace with the task at hand, despite the confusion caused by the Muslim League's ambivalent position on participating in the Assembly: 'We desire to proceed with the work as fast as possible, understanding very well the difficulties of the Muslim League members in the way of their coming and joining us at this stage. Let them think it over. Let us give them ample time to come. But that does not mean that we stop our work, that we stop thinking, that we stop doing anything whatsoever, until they make up their minds. That would lead to indefinite postponement. Hence, Sir, I have no hesitation in recommending this Resolution that we should appoint this Committee of twelve members as proposed.' C. Rajagopalachari, Constituent Assembly Debates, Vol. II, 25 January 1947.
14. Shiva Rao (ed.), *The Framing of India's Constitution: Select Documents*, Vol. II (Indian Institute of Public Administration 1967), 729.

15. B. Shiva Rao (ed.), *The Framing of India's Constitution: Select Documents,* Vol. II (Indian Institute of Public Administration 1967), 729.
16. Granville Austin, *The Indian Constitution: Cornerstone of a Nation* (Clarendon Press 1966), 193.
17. B. Shiva Rao (ed.), *The Framing of India's Constitution: Select Documents,* Vol. II (Indian Institute of Public Administration 1967), 553.
18. Section 102, Government of India Act, 1935, granted the governor-general of India the power to declare an emergency and allow the federal legislature to make laws on any subject, federal or provincial. Here, the legislative power of the governor-general was coextensive with that of the federal legislature.
19. T.T. Krishnamachari, Constituent Assembly Debates, Vol. IX, 2 August 1949.
20. B. Shiva Rao (ed.), *The Framing of India's Constitution: Select Documents,* Vol. III (Indian Institute of Public Administration 1967), 512.
21. Kazi Syed Karimuddin, Constituent Assembly Debates, Vol. IX, 2 August 1949.
22. *Emperor v Keshav Talpade, BOMLR*, Vol. 46 (1944): 22.
23. H.V. Kamath, Constituent Assembly Debates, Vol. IX, 20 August 1949.
24. Brajeshwar Prasad, Constituent Assembly Debates, Vol. IX, 2 August 1949.
25. B.R. Ambedkar, Constituent Assembly Debates, Vol. IX, 20 August 1949.

26. Krishna Chandra Sharma, Constituent Assembly Debates, Vol. IX, 20 August 1949.
27. Shibban Lal Saksena, Constituent Assembly Debates, Vol. IX, 20 August 1949.
28. Hriday Nath Kunzru, Constituent Assembly Debates, Vol. IX, 3 August 1949.
29. H.V. Kamath, Constituent Assembly Debates, Vol. IX, 20 August 1949.

FOUR: Bharat

1. M.K. Gandhi, *Hind Swaraj or Indian Home Rule* (first published 1909), 27.
2. M.K. Gandhi, *Hind Swaraj or Indian Home Rule* (first published 1909), 55.
3. *Collected Works of Mahatma Gandhi*, Vol. 30, 53.
4. M.K. Gandhi, *Constructive Programme: Its Meaning and Place* (first published 1941).
5. M.K. Gandhi, *Constructive Programme: Its Meaning and Place* (first published 1941), 5.
6. *Collected Works of Mahatma Gandhi*, Vol. 83, 113–14.
7. *Collected Works of Mahatma Gandhi*, Vol. 83, 113–14.
8. Narendra Chapalgaonkar, *Mahatma Gandhi and the Indian Constitution* (Routledge 2016), 105.
9. *Collected Works of Mahatma Gandhi*, Vol. 83, 113–14.
10. *Collected Works of Mahatma Gandhi*, Vol. 91, 371.
11. Annual Register Office, *The Indian Annual Register: January to June 1931*, Vol. I, 277.

12. Wesley Newcomb Hohfeld, 'Fundamental Legal Conceptions as Applied in Judicial Reasoning', *The Yale Law Journal*, Vol. 26, no. 8 (1917).
13. *Collected Works of Mahatma Gandhi*, Vol. 30, 53.
14. *Collected Works of Mahatma Gandhi*, Vol. 61, 348.
15. *Collected Works of Mahatma Gandhi*, Vol. 61, 348.
16. See Shruti Kapila, *Violent Fraternity: Indian Political Thought in the Global Age* (Princeton University Press 2021), 7.
17. *Collected Works of Mahatma Gandhi*, Vol. 52, 120.
18. *Collected Works of Mahatma Gandhi*, Vol. 52, 121.
19. Apa Pant, *An Unusual Raja: Mahatma Gandhi and the Aundh Experiment* (Sangam Books 1989), 11.
20. Apa Pant, *An Unusual Raja: Mahatma Gandhi and the Aundh Experiment* (Sangam Books 1989), 47; *Collected Works of Mahatma Gandhi*, Vol. 79, 90.
21. *Collected Works of Mahatma Gandhi*, Vol. 74, 190.
22. Narendra Chapalgaonkar, *Mahatma Gandhi and the Indian Constitution* (Routledge 2016), 70.
23. Narendra Chapalgaonkar, *Mahatma Gandhi and the Indian Constitution* (Routledge 2016), 71–72.
24. Apa Pant, *An Unusual Raja: Mahatma Gandhi and the Aundh Experiment* (Sangam Books 1989), 83–84.
25. *Collected Works of Mahatma Gandhi*, Vol. 74, 408.
26. Narendra Chapalgaonkar, *Mahatma Gandhi and the Indian Constitution* (Routledge 2016), 71–72.
27. *Collected Works of Mahatma Gandhi*, Vol. 74, 408.
28. *Collected Works of Mahatma Gandhi*, Vol. 74, 190.
29. Shriman Narayan Agarwal was a member of the Congress and the Constituent Assembly. He was also an educationist;

he was part of educational bodies such as the All India Board of Technical Studies and Business Administration, and served as the Dean of the Faculty of Commerce, Nagpur University. Post-Independence, he was a member of the Planning Commission, Government of India. Parliament Secretariat, *Parliament of India – House of the People: Who's Who* (1952), 4–5.

30. Shriman Narayan Agarwal, *Gandhian Constitution for Free India* (Kitabistan 1946), 39.
31. Shriman Narayan Agarwal, *Gandhian Constitution for Free India* (Kitabistan 1946), 69.
32. Shriman Narayan Agarwal, *Gandhian Constitution for Free India* (Kitabistan 1946), 79.
33. Shriman Narayan Agarwal, *Gandhian Constitution for Free India* (Kitabistan 1946), 4.
34. *Collected Works of Mahatma Gandhi*, Vol. 88, 200.
35. *Collected Works of Mahatma Gandhi*, Vol. 42, 380.
36. *Collected Works of Mahatma Gandhi*, Vol. 42, 446.
37. Annual Register Office, *The Indian Annual Register: January to June 1931*, Vol. I, 277.
38. Annual Register Office, *The Indian Annual Register: January to June 1940*, Vol. I, 232–34.
39. *Collected Works of Mahatma Gandhi*, Vol. 77, 113.
40. *Collected Works of Mahatma Gandhi*, Vol. 77, 113.
41. *Collected Works of Mahatma Gandhi*, Vol. 77, 114.
42. *Collected Works of Mahatma Gandhi*, Vol. 93, 148.
43. Kengal Hanumanthaiah, Constituent Assembly Debates, Vol. XI, 17 November 1949.

44. Kengal Hanumanthaiah, Constituent Assembly Debates, Vol. XI, 17 November 1949.
45. Apa Pant, *An Unusual Raja: Mahatma Gandhi and the Aundh Experiment* (Sangam Books 1989), 81.
46. Shankarrao Deo, Constituent Assembly Debates, Vol. XI, 21 November 1949.
47. Shankarrao Deo, Constituent Assembly Debates, Vol. XI, 21 November 1949.

FIVE: Hindusthan

1. Annual Register Office, *The Indian Annual Register: January to June 1940*, Vol. I, 277.
2. Annual Register Office, *The Indian Annual Register: January to June 1941*, Vol. I, 278.
3. Barbara D. Metcalf and Thomas R. Metcalf, *A Concise History of Modern India* (Third edition, Cambridge University Press 2012), 161.
4. Barbara D. Metcalf and Thomas R. Metcalf, *A Concise History of Modern India* (Third edition, Cambridge University Press 2012), 161.
5. Dhananjay Keer, *Veer Savarkar* (Second edition, Popular Prakashan 1966), 91.
6. V.D. Savarkar, *Essentials of Hindutva* (Fifth edition, Veer Savarkar Prakashan 1923), 89.
7. Walter Andersen, 'The Rashtriya Swayamsevak Sangh: II: Who Represents the Hindus?', *Economic and Political Weekly*, Vol. 7, no. 12 (1972): 633, 638.

8. Enayetur Rahim and Joyce L. Rahim, *Bengal Politics: Documents of the Raj: Vol. II* (The University Press Limited 1999), 127; Chhanda Chatterjee, *Syama Prasad Mookerjee, the Hindu Dissent and the Partition of Bengal: 1932–1947* (Routledge 2021), 211; Chanchal Adhikary, 'Upendra Nath Barman and Caste Politics Among the Rajbanshis of North Bengal', *Voice of Dalit*, Vol. 6, no. 2 (2013): 137, 142.
9. Annual Register Office, *The Indian Annual Register: January to June 1941*, Vol. I, 280.
10. He was also the advocate for Savarkar in the Gandhi murder trial. Kanika Sharma, 'Spectacular Justice: Aesthetics and Power in the Gandhi Murder Trial' in Awol Allo (ed.), *The Courtroom as a Space of Resistance: Reflections on the Legacy of the Rivonia Trial* (Routledge 2016), 340.
11. The members of the committee were D.V. Gokhale, L.B. Bhopatkar, K.V. Kelkar, and M.R. Dhamdhere. *The Constitution of the Hindusthan Free State Act 1944* (Loksangraha Press).
12. Foreword, *The Constitution of the Hindusthan Free State Act 1944* (Loksangraha Press), 24.
13. *The Constitution of the Hindusthan Free State Act 1944* (Loksangraha Press), 1.
14. For details, see Christophe Jaffrelot, *Religion, Caste & Politics in India* (Primus Books 2010).
15. The Four Freedoms are the freedom from want, the freedom from fear, the freedom of expression, and the freedom of worship. *The Constitution of the Hindusthan Free State Act 1944* (Loksangraha Press), 9.

16. *The Constitution of the Hindusthan Free State Act 1944* (Loksangraha Press), 7.
17. Foreword, *The Constitution of the Hindusthan Free State Act 1944* (Loksangraha Press), 24.
18. Eesvan Krishnan, 'Land Acquisition in British India c. 1894–1927' (DPhil thesis, University of Oxford 2014), 20.
19. Walter Andersen, 'The Rashtriya Swayamsevak Sangh: II: Who Represents the Hindus?', *Economic and Political Weekly*, Vol. 7, no. 12 (1972): 633, 637.
20. National Archives of India, Abhilekh Patal Portal for Access to Archives and Learning, 'Note on the organisation, aims etc. of the Rashtriya Swayam Sewak Sangh', Home Department (Political), File No. 28/8/42-Poll (I), 11.
21. Christophe Jaffrelot, *The Hindu Nationalist Movement and Indian Politics: 1925 to the 1990s: Strategies of Identity-building, Implantation and Mobilisation (with Special Reference to Central India)* (Penguin Books India 1999), 35.
22. Christophe Jaffrelot, *The Hindu Nationalist Movement and Indian Politics: 1925 to the 1990s: Strategies of Identity-building, Implantation and Mobilisation (with Special Reference to Central India)* (Penguin Books India 1999), 73–74.
23. National Archives of India, Abhilekh Patal Portal for Access to Archives and Learning, 'Note on the organisation, aims etc. of the Rashtriya Swayam Sewak Sangh', Home Department (Political), File No. 28/8/42-Poll (I), 9.
24. Nathuram Godse was one of the founder members of the Hindu Rashtra Dal. Namrata M. Ganneri, '"Whither Hindu Unity?" – Unravelling the RSS–Hindu Mahasabha Relationship: Perspectives from Maharashtra', *Proceedings of the Indian History Congress*, Vol. 76 (2015): 467, 475.

25. National Archives of India, Abhilekh Patal Portal for Access to Archives and Learning, 'Note on the organisation, aims etc. of the Rashtriya Swayam Sewak Sangh', Home Department (Political), File No. 28/8/42-Poll (I), 10.
26. Annual Register Office, *The Indian Annual Register: July to December 1944*, Vol. II, 203–04.
27. Letter from L.B. Bhopatkar (Acting President, All India Hindu Mahasabha) to the Cabinet Delegation, 15 April 1946, S.P. Mookerjee Papers, Sub-File No. 65, Nehru Memorial Museum and Library, New Delhi.
28. Telegram from Jankibai Joshi (President, All India Hindu Women's Conference) to Sardar Vallabhbhai Patel, Jawaharlal Nehru, Sardar Baldev Singh, Rajendra Prasad, Sarat Chandra Bose, and M.K. Gandhi, 9 October 1946, S.P. Mookerjee Papers, Sub-File No. 65, Nehru Memorial Museum and Library, New Delhi.
29. There was some discussion on referendum and recall, but it made little headway. K.T. Shah, Constituent Assembly Debates, Vol. VII; H.V. Kamath, Constituent Assembly Debates, Vol. VIII; H.V. Kamath, Constituent Assembly Debates, Vol. VIII.
30. *The Constitution of the Hindusthan Free State Act 1944* (Loksangraha Press), 34.
31. Shyama Prasad Mookerjee, Constituent Assembly Debates, Vol. I, 17 December 1946.
32. The Socialist Party of India prepared a draft constitution, entitled the 'Draft Constitution of the Indian Republic', in 1948, which aimed to establish the foundation of a socialist economy in India. Niraja Gopal Jayal, *Citizenship and Its*

Discontents: An Indian History (Harvard University Press 2013), 143.

33. Narhar Vishnu Gadgil, Constituent Assembly Debates, Vol. XI, 18 November 1949.

SIX: India

1. *Dr Babasaheb Ambedkar: Books and Writings*, Vol. 12 (Dr Ambedkar Foundation, Ministry of Social Justice and Empowerment, Government of India, 2020), 665–70.
2. B. Pattabhi Sitaramayya, Constituent Assembly Debates, Vol. XI, 25 November 1949.
3. Rajendra Prasad, Constituent Assembly Debates, Vol. XI, 26 November 1949.
4. Lord Bingham of Cornhill, Lord Chief Justice of England and Wales, 'Law Day Lecture' (Speech on the Occasion of the Golden Jubilee Celebrations of the Supreme Court of India, New Delhi, 26 November 1999) (2000), SCC, Vol. 1 (2000): 29.
5. Hugo Gorringe, 'Ambedkar Icons: Whys and Wherefores' in Anand Teltumbde and Suraj Yengde (eds), *The Radical in Ambedkar: Critical Reflections* (Penguin Books 2018).
6. Sambhaji Bhagat, 'माझा भीम मले भेटतो बाई, मले सांगतो काही ', YouTube, 10 June 2022, https://www.youtube.com/watch?v=yJKjhG-xy6Y.
7. B.R. Ambedkar, Constituent Assembly Debates, Vol. XI, 25 November 1949.
8. B.R. Ambedkar, Constituent Assembly Debates, Vol. I, 17 December 1946.

9. B.R. Ambedkar, Constituent Assembly Debates, Vol. I, 17 December 1946.
10. B.R. Ambedkar, Constituent Assembly Debates, Vol. I, 17 December 1946.
11. Sarojini Naidu, Constituent Assembly Debates, Vol. I, 11 December 1946.
12. There were several other committees, including ad hoc committees and sub-committees, which were constituted. B. Shiva Rao (ed.), *The Framing of India's Constitution: Select Documents*, Vols. I–IV (Indian Institute of Public Administration 1966–68).
13. Ambedkar was part of the Committee on the Functions of the Constituent Assembly, the Ad-Hoc Committee on the Supreme Court, the Sub-Committee on Minority Problems affecting East Punjab and West Bengal, the Ad-Hoc Committee on National Flag, the Sub-Committee on Amendment, Sub-Committee I on the Procedure for the Election of the President of the Union, and Sub-Committee II on the Composition of the Council of States. B. Shiva Rao (ed.), *The Framing of India's Constitution: Select Documents*, Vols. I–IV (Indian Institute of Public Administration 1966–68).
14. B. Shiva Rao (ed.), *The Framing of India's Constitution: Select Documents*, Vol. II (Indian Institute of Public Administration 1967), 84.
15. See Chapter 1.
16. B. Shiva Rao (ed.), *The Framing of India's Constitution: Select Documents*, Vol. II (Indian Institute of Public Administration 1967), 116.

17. B. Shiva Rao (ed.), *The Framing of India's Constitution: Select Documents*, Vol. II (Indian Institute of Public Administration 1967), 183.
18. Constituent Assembly Debates, Vol. V, 29 August 1947.
19. Bidyut Chakrabarty, *The Socio-political Ideas of BR Ambedkar: Liberal Constitutionalism in a Creative Mould* (Routledge 2019), viii.
20. National Archives of India, Abhilekh Patal Portal for Access to Archives and Learning, 'Election of Members of Constituent Assembly', Digitized Private Papers of Dr Rajendra Prasad, File No. 1-E/47 17–18; Granville Austin, *The Indian Constitution: Cornerstone of a Nation* (Clarendon Press 1966), 13.
21. Bidyut Chakrabarty, *The Socio-political Ideas of BR Ambedkar: Liberal Constitutionalism in a Creative Mould* (Routledge 2019), 93.
22. Bidyut Chakrabarty, *The Socio-political Ideas of BR Ambedkar: Liberal Constitutionalism in a Creative Mould* (Routledge 2019), viii; Harold Coward (ed.), *Indian Critiques of Gandhi* (State University of New York Press 2003), 63.
23. B. Shiva Rao (ed.), *The Framing of India's Constitution: Select Documents*, Vol. III (Indian Institute of Public Administration 1967), 316.
24. B.R. Ambedkar, Constituent Assembly Debates, Vol. XI, 25 November 1949.
25. Surendra Nath Mukherjee was the Joint Secretary of the Constituent Assembly Secretariat and the Chief Draftsman of the Constituent Assembly. Ornit Shani, *How India Became Democratic: Citizenship and the Making of the*

Universal Franchise (Cambridge University Press 2017), 180–81, 201–03.

26. B.R. Ambedkar, Constituent Assembly Debates, Vol. XI, 25 November 1949.
27. B. Shiva Rao (ed.), *The Framing of India's Constitution: Select Documents*, Vol. III (Indian Institute of Public Administration 1967), 248–52.
28. B. Shiva Rao (ed.), *The Framing of India's Constitution: Select Documents*, Vol. III (Indian Institute of Public Administration 1967), 514.
29. K.T. Shah, Constituent Assembly Debates, Vol. VII, 17 November 1948.
30. B.R. Ambedkar, Constituent Assembly Debates, Vol. VII, 29 November 1948.
31. Dhananjay Keer, *Dr Ambedkar: Life and Mission* (Third edition, Popular Prakashan 1954), 27.
32. J. Krishnamurty, 'Ambedkar's Educational Odyssey, 1913–1927', *Journal of Social Inclusion Studies*, Vol. 5, no. 2 (2019): 147, 149.
33. *Dr Babasaheb Ambedkar: Books and Writings* (Dr Ambedkar Foundation, Ministry of Social Justice and Empowerment, Government of India, 2020), Vol. 12, 673.
34. J. Krishnamurty, 'Ambedkar's Educational Odyssey, 1913–1927', Journal of Social Inclusion Studies, Vol. 5, no. 2 (2019): 147, 150.
35. Dhananjay Keer, *Dr Ambedkar: Life and Mission* (Third edition, Popular Prakashan 1954), 28–31.
36. While there were several other professors he worked with closely in both America and England, it was Dewey whose

influence is most significant when it comes to Ambedkar's political positions. Arun P. Mukherjee, 'B.R. Ambedkar, John Dewey, and the Meaning of Democracy', *New Literacy History*, Vol. 40, no. 2 (2009): 345.

37. John Dewey, *Democracy and Education: An Introduction to the Philosophy of Education* (The Macmillan Company 1916), 101.
38. John Dewey, *Democracy and Education: An Introduction to the Philosophy of Education* (The Macmillan Company 1916), 101.
39. *Dr Babasaheb Ambedkar: Books and Writings*, Vol. 10 (Dr Ambedkar Foundation, Ministry of Social Justice and Empowerment, Government of India, 2020), 41.
40. *Dr Babasaheb Ambedkar: Books and Writings*, Vol. 12 (Dr Ambedkar Foundation, Ministry of Social Justice and Empowerment, Government of India, 2020), 673–78.
41. *Dr Babasaheb Ambedkar: Books and Writings*, Vol. 12 (Dr Ambedkar Foundation, Ministry of Social Justice and Empowerment, Government of India, 2020), 677–78.
42. *Dr Babasaheb Ambedkar: Books and Writings*, Vol. 1 (Dr Ambedkar Foundation, Ministry of Social Justice and Empowerment, Government of India, 2020), 271.
43. *Dr Babasaheb Ambedkar: Books and Writings*, Vol. 1 (Dr Ambedkar Foundation, Ministry of Social Justice and Empowerment, Government of India, 2020), 353.
44. *Dr Babasaheb Ambedkar: Books and Writings*, Vol. 1 (Dr Ambedkar Foundation, Ministry of Social Justice and Empowerment, Government of India, 2020) 313.
45. B.R. Ambedkar, Speech in the 5th Plenary Meeting (Indian Round Table Conference [First Session], London, 20 November 1930), 136.

46. *Dr Babasaheb Ambedkar: Books and Writings*, Vol. 2 (Dr Ambedkar Foundation, Ministry of Social Justice and Empowerment, Government of India, 2020), 382–85.
47. *Dr Babasaheb Ambedkar: Books and Writings*, Vol. 2 (Dr Ambedkar Foundation, Ministry of Social Justice and Empowerment, Government of India, 2020), 385.
48. *Dr Babasaheb Ambedkar: Books and Writings*, Vol. 2 (Dr Ambedkar Foundation, Ministry of Social Justice and Empowerment, Government of India, 2020), 513
49. *Dr Babasaheb Ambedkar: Books and Writings*, Vol. 17, Part III (Dr Ambedkar Foundation, Ministry of Social Justice and Empowerment, Government of India, 2020), 49.
50. *Dr Babasaheb Ambedkar: Books and Writings*, Vol. 17, Part III (Dr Ambedkar Foundation, Ministry of Social Justice and Empowerment, Government of India, 2020), 212.
51. *Dr Babasaheb Ambedkar: Books and Writings*, Vol. 5 (Dr Ambedkar Foundation, Ministry of Social Justice and Empowerment, Government of India, 2020), 289.
52. M.K. Gandhi, Speech at the 10th Meeting of the Minorities Committee (Indian Round Table Conference [Second Session], London, 15 November 1931), 1384.
53. M.K. Gandhi, Speech at the 10th Meeting of the Minorities Committee (Indian Round Table Conference [Second Session], London, 15 November 1931), 1384.
54. Annual Register Office, *The Indian Annual Register: July to December 1932*, Vol. II, 233–37.
55. M.K. Gandhi, Speech at the 10th Meeting of the Minorities Committee (Indian Round Table Conference Second Session, London, 15 November 1931), 1382.

56. *Dr Babasaheb Ambedkar: Books and Writings*, Vol. 5 (Dr Ambedkar Foundation, Ministry of Social Justice and Empowerment, Government of India, 2020), 333.
57. *Dr Babasaheb Ambedkar: Books and Writings*, Vol. 5 (Dr Ambedkar Foundation, Ministry of Social Justice and Empowerment, Government of India, 2020), 328.
58. *Collected Works of Mahatma Gandhi*, Vol. 56, 347.
59. *Dr Babasaheb Ambedkar: Books and Writings*, Vol. 5 (Dr Ambedkar Foundation, Ministry of Social Justice and Empowerment, Government of India, 2020), 341.
60. *Collected Works of Mahatma Gandhi*, Vol. 57 (Gandhi Sevagram Ashram 1981), 444–46.
61. Annual Register Office, *The Indian Annual Register: July to December 1932*, Vol. II, 255–56.
62. Ravinder Kumar, 'Gandhi, Ambedkar and the Poona Pact, 1932', *South Asia: Journal of South Asian Studies*, Vol. 8, nos. 1 and 2 (1985): 87, 99.
63. *Collected Works of Mahatma Gandhi*, Vol. 59, 227.
64. *Dr Babasaheb Ambedkar: Books and Writings*, Vol. 5 (Dr Ambedkar Foundation, Ministry of Social Justice and Empowerment, Government of India, 2020), 343.
65. B.R. Ambedkar, *Mr Gandhi and the Emancipation of the Untouchables* (Bheem Patrika Publications 1943), 27.
66. *Dr Babasaheb Ambedkar: Books and Writings*, Vol. 5, (Dr Ambedkar Foundation, Ministry of Social Justice and Empowerment, Government of India, 2020), 347.
67. Sections 12(3), 60(5), 130(3), 226, Draft Constitution (Constitutional Adviser, B.N. Rau). B. Shiva Rao (ed.),

The Framing of India's Constitution: Select Documents, Vol. III (Indian Institute of Public Administration 1967), 4–197.

68. D.R. Nagaraj, *The Flaming Feet and Other Essays: The Dalit Movement in India* (Second edition, Permanent Black 2010), 208.
69. Dhananjay Keer, *Dr Ambedkar: Life and Mission* (Third edition, Popular Prakashan 1954), 449.
70. B.R. Ambedkar, Rajya Sabha Official Debates, 2 September 1953, 874.

Epilogue: Inflection Point

1. 'English rendering of PM's address in the 8th Episode of "Mann Ki Baat 2.0" on 26.01.2020', Press Information Bureau, 26 January 2020.

Acknowledgements

Thanking those who have contributed to this book in this acknowledgements section is an altogether insufficient way of expressing how grateful I am to them. But a better method has not yet been devised, and till that happens, this must do.

This book was primarily written during the pandemic when we were all locked down in our homes in an atmosphere of fear and uncertainty. Dhvani, my wife, and Shruti, my sister-in-law, made that difficult time pleasant with endless games of Catan, improvised table tennis on the dining table, and a happy routine of shared household chores (they took over the lion's share, while I wrote). In the midst of this, Dhvani found time to read multiple drafts, provide comments, and make this book the best version of itself it could be. I couldn't ask for more.

I have been developing the intellectual foundation for the arguments that are made in the book in my newspaper columns for the *Times of India* and the *Telegraph* over the last decade. Many thanks to my editors Jaideep Bose, Swagato Ganguly, Saubhik Chakrabarti, and Uddalak Mukherjee for indulging me for so many years. One such editor, Parth Mehrotra, formerly at the *Indian Express* and now at Juggernaut, saw in my writing the makings of a 'trade book' and asked me to take a shot. This book would not have been possible without Parth's leap of faith, infinite patience, and deft editing. It has been a joy to work with him and his excellent team at Juggernaut.

Raag Yadava and Shivprasad Swaminathan have been fellow travellers on this journey. I have benefited from many conversations with them on the need to develop a system of law and legal education that works for India. We have collectively felt an urgent need to decolonize our Constitution, our legal system, and our legal education. This is not to decry a colonial system for the fact of it being colonial, but rather to point out how in certain respects it may be entirely unsuited to India. B.N. Srikrishna, Bibek Debroy, Ireena Vittal, Jasti Chelameswar, Nandan Nilekani, and Uday Shankar have inspired me, in their own ways, to be bold and original in my thinking. I hope I have translated some of that originality into this book.

A book lies as much in its ideas as in its execution. Aditya Prasanna Bhattacharya spent sleepless nights researching the history of the Constitution prior to Independence including coming up with a wonderfully succinct timeline of events. Kadambari Agarwal made a semi-permanent home for herself in the Nehru Memorial Library digging up old papers and hunting for archival sources. Aditya and Kadambari are the pillars on which this book stands, ably supported by Shraddha Paikray, Ishika Garg, and Anjali Singh.

I would like to thank all my colleagues and friends at the Vidhi Centre for Legal Policy for giving me the time and freedom over the last few years to conceptualize and write this book. Ujaan, my son, gave me neither of these things. But unknowingly, he gave me something more precious: the determination to complete this book so that future generations of Indians and formerly colonized people can think for themselves about their laws, institutions, and constitutions. I hope someday he will read it.